50 Sunflowers
TO KNIT, CROCHET & FELT

D1439276

50 Sunflowers
TO KNIT, CROCHET & FELT

Kristin Nicholas

Search Press

A QUARTO BOOK

Published in 2013 by Search Press Ltd
Wellwood
North Farm Road
Tunbridge Wells
Kent TN2 3DR

ISBN: 978-1-84448-900-8

Conceived, designed and produced by
Quarto Publishing plc
The Old Brewery
6 Blundell Street
London N7 9BH

QUA: FSEK

Project editor: Michelle Pickering
Pattern editor: Betty Barnden
Art director: Caroline Guest
Designer: Karin Skånberg
Design assistant: Nadine Resch
Crochet charts: Betty Barnden, Kuo Kang Chen
Photographers: Nicky Dowey (projects),
Phil Wilkins (flowers)
Indexer: Dorothy Frame

Creative director: Moira Clinch
Publisher: Paul Carslake

Colour separation by PICA Digital Pte Ltd, Singapore
Printed by 1010 Printing International Ltd, China

Safety note
Sunflowers and other designs that are stiffened with
wire, incorporate hair grips or are decorated with
beads are not suitable for babies and young children.
When making items for youngsters, always use top-
quality, clean stuffing marked as suitable for toys, and
sew on any small parts (such as petals) very securely.

CONTENTS

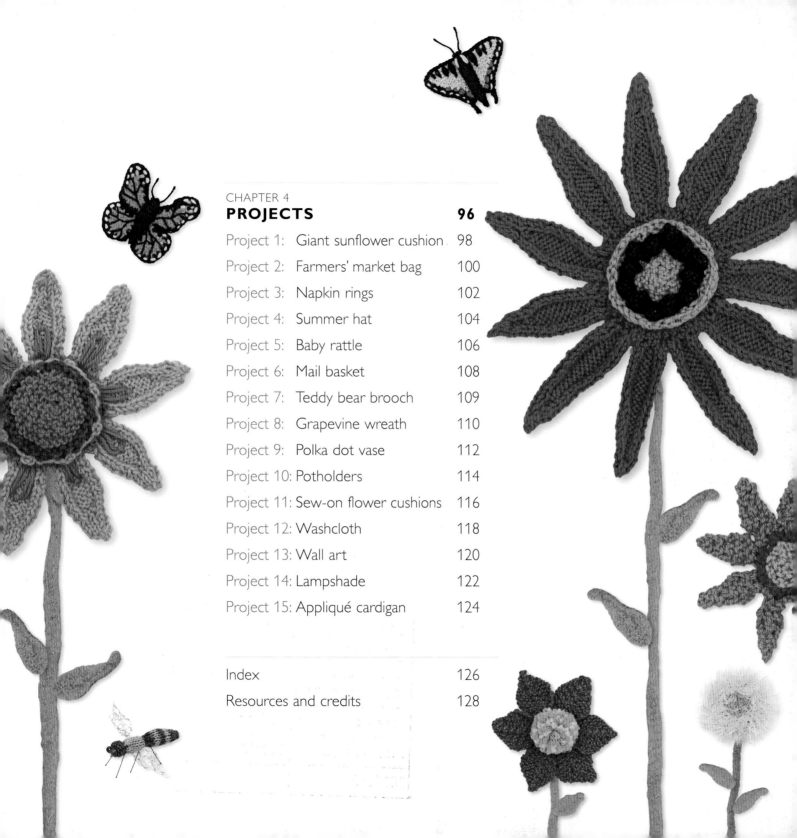

CHAPTER 4
PROJECTS 96

FOREWORD

At our New England farm, my family grows over fifteen varieties of sunflower every summer.
The growing season doesn't last long, so to tide over my lack of real flowers until the next
season's blooms, I began knitting, crocheting and felting sunflowers to decorate our home
and clothes. Having this sunny motif with us through the winter makes the house feel warm
and cosy. Now you too can make yourself a bouquet of cheerful sunflowers. In this book
you'll find many different styles. Sunflowers grow in many colours, so don't restrict yourself
to yellows and golds. Once you get going, you'll be able to tweak the instructions to design your
own flowers. Most of all, have lots of fun stitching these beautiful blooms. Spread the sunflower love!

Kristin Nicholas

ABOUT THIS BOOK

This book provides a stunning selection of 50 sunflowers, leaves, stems
and small creatures to knit and crochet. Each of these gorgeous creations
can be used to embellish garments, gifts, accessories and much more.

CHAPTER 1: **BEFORE YOU BEGIN**
(pages 8–31)

The book begins with some useful information about
yarns, needles, hooks, abbreviations and chart symbols,
as well as some notes on how to work some key
knitting and crochet techniques – much of the
know-how you need to get started.

CHAPTER 2: **DIRECTORY**
(pages 32–49)

The directory is a showcase of all the beautiful designs
featured in this book. Look through this colourful visual
guide, select your design and then turn to the relevant
page of instructions to create your chosen piece.

*Each design is shown in proportion to the others on
the spread, which gives an idea of size and scale.*

*Each item is labelled with a number that
corresponds to the relevant pattern in the
instructions chapter (pages 50–95).*

CHAPTER 3: **INSTRUCTIONS**
(pages 50–95)

Organised into separate knitting and crochet sections, here you will find instructions on how to create every design featured in the directory. All of the knitted designs are explained with clearly written patterns, while the crochet designs are explained with both charts and written instructions, so you can use either method or, better still, combine both.

LEVEL OF DIFFICULTY

Each design is accompanied by a symbol indicating the pattern's degree of difficulty.

Knitting   *Crochet*

Basic

Intermediate

Advanced

CHAPTER 4: **PROJECTS**
(pages 96–125)

All of the designs featured in this book can be used to embellish and make a number of items, from hats and bags to cushions and home accessories. This chapter presents a selection of ideas to inspire and encourage you to use the designs in a variety of ways.

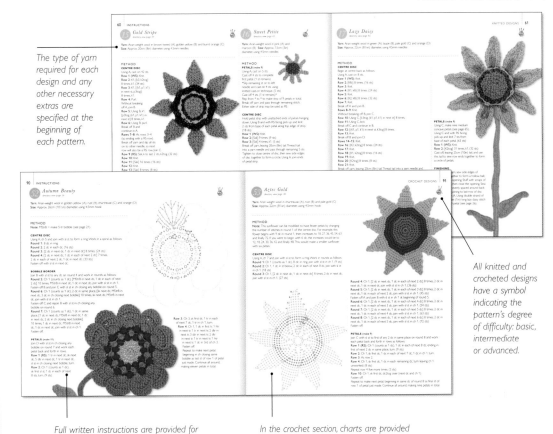

The type of yarn required for each design and any other necessary extras are specified at the beginning of each pattern.

All knitted and crocheted designs have a symbol indicating the pattern's degree of difficulty: basic, intermediate or advanced.

Full written instructions are provided for each knitted and crocheted design.

In the crochet section, charts are provided to amplify the written instructions.

PROJECT 11:
SEW-ON FLOWER CUSHIONS

Liven up some plain cushions by decorating them with sunflowers. Sew a selection of knit and crochet sunflowers, stems and leaves randomly on to the front of a cushion, or make a bold statement with a single large bloom in a vibrant colour scheme. Use sewing thread in matching colours to attach the flowers, making sure that the ends of stems are tucked under them. Take care to keep the back of the cushion loose from the front when sewing.

Each project is illustrated with a photograph of the finished item.

Inspirational ideas on how to apply your knitted and crocheted designs are provided.

BEFORE YOU BEGIN

Before you get started, here is some useful information about yarns, needles, hooks, abbreviations and chart symbols, as well as some notes to help you brush up on your knitting and crochet skills.

MATERIALS AND EQUIPMENT

Few materials and minimal craft skills are needed for the designs featured in this book. Obviously, changing the type of yarn and colour will produce a different result and scale, so it can be very rewarding to experiment.

YARNS

Yarns are available in a range of weights, from fine to chunky, and this will affect the finished size of the flower (or other design) that you are making. You should also be aware of the properties of different yarn fibres, from the fullness of cotton to the elasticity of wool, because the construction of a yarn will affect its behaviour and characteristics, and so will influence the end result. There are also many fancy and novelty yarns to experiment with, from highly textured fringed yarn (also known as fur or eyelash yarn) to absorbent kitchen cotton yarn for making accessories such as washcloths. Since yarns may vary from one manufacturer to another, only generic yarn types are indicated in the patterns in this book.

KNITTING NEEDLES

Vary the size of knitting needles according to the yarn you are using, as recommended on the ball band of the yarn. Pairs of knitting needles are made in a variety of lengths and materials, including aluminium, plastic, bamboo and wood. For most of the designs in this book, a conventional pair of needles is used, but two double-pointed needles are needed to make an i-cord, and four double-pointed needles are used for knitting in the round.

A variety of
different yarn
types and weights.

Pairs of knitting
needles and sets
of double-pointed
needles in various
materials and sizes.

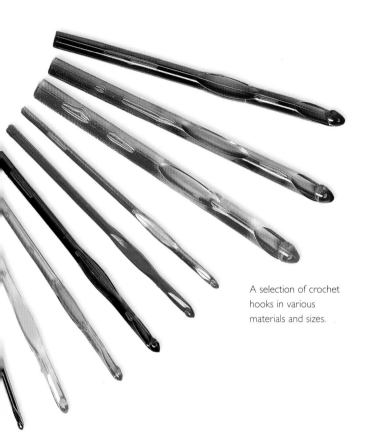

A selection of crochet hooks in various materials and sizes.

CROCHET HOOKS

Crochet hooks are available in a wide range of sizes and materials. Most hooks are made from aluminium or plastic. Small sizes of steel hooks are made for working with very fine yarns. Hand-made wooden, bamboo and horn hooks are also available. Choosing a hook is largely a matter of personal preference. The design of the hook affects the ease of working considerably. Look for a hook that has a comfortable grip. Hook sizes are quoted differently in Europe and the United States, and some brands of hooks are labelled with more than one type of numbering.

ADJUSTING SIZE

The finished size of a sunflower (or other design) will depend on the yarn and needles or hook that you choose; as a rule, use the needle/hook size recommended on the yarn ball band. However, it is possible to change the size of a design slightly by using needles or a hook one or two sizes smaller or larger than recommended.

ADDITIONAL EQUIPMENT

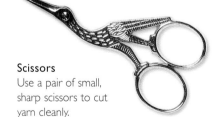

Yarn needles

These are used for sewing seams and for weaving in yarn ends. Yarn needles have blunt tips to avoid splitting stitches. They are available in different sizes. Choose a yarn needle to suit the weight of your yarn; the eye should be large enough for the yarn to pass through easily.

Markers and row counters

Some designs call for the use of a marker to indicate a stitch or row, or an edge that is being shaped. The marker should be removed after the piece is complete. You can use a safety pin, a split ring marker or a short length of contrasting yarn tied in place. Similarly, a row counter may help you to keep track of the number of rows or rounds you have worked.

Scissors

Use a pair of small, sharp scissors to cut yarn cleanly.

NOTES ON KNITTING

This section is not a lesson in knitting. It is simply a list of the abbreviations used in this book, together with a quick refresher on some of the techniques used in the patterns.

ABBREVIATIONS

beg	begin(ning)	MB3	make 3-st bobble (see page 15)	st(s)	stitch(es)
cdd	centre double decrease: slip 2 stitches as if to knit 2 together, knit next stitch, then pass both slipped stitches over knitted stitch and off needle	MB5	make 5-st bobble (see page 15)	tog	together
		MP	make petal (see page 15)	w&t	wrap and turn (see page 14)
				WS	wrong side of work
dpn	double-pointed needle(s)	p	purl	yo	wrap yarn over needle (anticlockwise) to make an extra stitch
k	knit	p2tog	purl 2 stitches (or number specified) together		
(k1, p1, k1) in next st	k1 in next stitch, keeping old stitch on left needle; p1 in same stitch, again keeping old stitch on left needle; k1 in same stitch and this time drop old stitch from left needle (3 sts made from 1 st)			*	asterisks mark a section of instructions to be repeated
		rem	remain(ing)	( )	round brackets indicate a group of stitches to be worked together
		rep	repeat		
k2tog	knit 2 stitches (or number specified) together	RS	right side of work	[ ]	work instructions in square brackets the number of times stated after the brackets
		sl	slip		
kfb	knit into front and back of same stitch	ssk	slip next stitch knitwise, slip following stitch knitwise, insert left needle into front loops of both slipped stitches and knit 2 together		
m1	make 1: lift horizontal strand in front of next stitch and knit into back of it				

SLIPKNOT

A slipknot forms the first stitch on the needle before casting on.

1 Loop the yarn around two fingers of your left hand, with the ball end on top. Dip the needle into the loop, catch the ball end of the yarn and pull it through the loop.

2 Pull the ends of the yarn to tighten the knot. Tighten the ball end to bring the knot up to the needle.

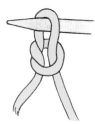

ENDS OF YARN

The end of yarn left after making the slipknot should be a reasonable length so that it can be used for sewing up. It can also be very useful for covering up imperfections, such as awkward colour changes. The same applies to the end left after casting off. Ends left when a new colour is joined in should be woven in along a seam or row end on the wrong side. In this book, the ends left at the tip of petals or leaves will be better woven in before the main sewing up.

CASTING ON

There are several cast-on methods, each with its own merits. Generally, you can use whichever method you prefer, but the following two techniques are specified in this book when stitches need to be added within the body of the knitting.

Knitted cast-on

This simple two-needle method is used to add stitches to those already on the left needle.

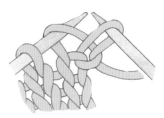

1 *Knit into the first stitch on the left needle, but do not slip the stitch off the left needle afterwards.

2 Transfer the new stitch from the right needle on to the left needle. Knitting into the new stitch each time, repeat from * until the required number of stitches has been cast on.

Loop cast-on

This method is used to add extra stitches on the right needle in the form of a series of loose loops. Loop the yarn around your thumb, then insert the needle into the loop. Slip your thumb out and gently pull the yarn to make a stitch on the needle. Repeat until you have the required number of stitches. Do not make the loops too tight.

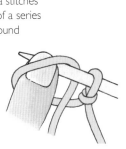

The knitted cast-on technique is used to make the swallowtails on this butterfly (page 68).

CASTING OFF

A simple knit stitch cast-off is used in this book unless specified otherwise. Knit two stitches. *With the left needle, lift the first stitch over the second and off the right needle. Knit the next stitch. Repeat from * until one stitch remains. Break off the yarn, pass the end through this stitch and tighten. When a row is only partially cast off, the count of stitches to be worked after the cast-off usually includes the stitch already on the right needle.

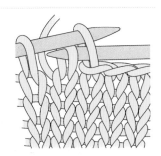

SLIP STITCHES

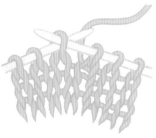

Many techniques involve slipping stitches from the left to the right needle without working them. To slip a stitch knitwise, insert the right needle into the stitch as if to knit it, but then slip the stitch off the left needle without knitting it. Use the same technique to slip a stitch purlwise (pictured), but insert the right needle into the stitch as if to purl it. As a rule of thumb, always slip stitches purlwise unless the instructions state otherwise. The exception is when a stitch is part of a decrease (such as ssk; page 12), in which case the stitches are slipped knitwise.

PICK UP AND KNIT

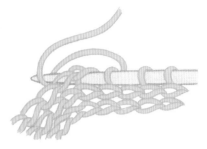

The pick up and knit technique involves knitting up new stitches along the edge of a knitted piece, ready to work in another direction. This avoids having to cast on a separate piece and join it with a seam. In this book, it is often used to join a series of petals into a long strip, ready to work the centre disc of the flower. With RS facing you, insert the right needle under an edge stitch, take the yarn around the needle and pull a loop through to make a stitch. Repeat for the number of stitches required, spacing the picked up stitches evenly along the edge. The next row will be a WS row.

KNITTING IN THE ROUND

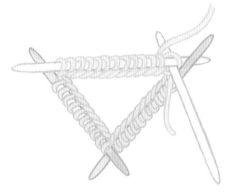

When knitting in the round using four double-pointed needles (dpn), the stitches are distributed among three of the needles and the spare needle is used to knit with. Bring the first and third needles together to form a circle and use the spare needle to work the stitches off the first (left) needle and on to the spare (right) needle in the usual way. This is done with the RS (outside) of the work facing you, unless stated otherwise. Take the yarn firmly from one double-pointed needle to the next or a ladder will appear.

WRAP AND TURN (w&t)

Short-row shaping is when you turn the needles partway through a row, leaving some of the stitches unworked. This wrap and turn technique can be used to prevent a hole from forming when making a mid-row turn.

1 Work the number of stitches required before the turn, take the yarn to the opposite side of the work, slip the next stitch purlwise from left to right needle and return the yarn to the original side of the work.

2 Slip the wrapped stitch back on to the left needle, turn and tension the yarn ready to work the next row.

The Robin (page 72) is knitted in the round and uses the wrap and turn technique.

YARN OVER (yo)

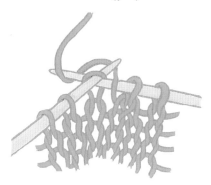

Taking the yarn over the needle makes a new stitch, and forms either a decorative hole below the stitch mid-row or a loop at the beginning of a row. Bring the yarn forwards under the right needle and then take it over the needle to be in position to work the next stitch. If this is a purl stitch, bring the yarn to the front again.

MAKE PETAL (MP)

This technique is used to create loose-edged, frilly petals. On a WS row and using the loop cast-on technique (see page 13), cast 5 sts (or number specified) on to the right needle. Turn the work and cast off the same number of stitches as were just cast on (count them as you lift them off). Leaving the petal just made towards you (at RS of work), bring the yarn between the needles towards you, slip the remaining stitch from the right needle on to the left needle and turn the work again so that the WS is facing you, ready to work the next stitch.

The make petal technique is used to create the frilly petals on Giant Sungold (page 54).

BOBBLES

Worked into a single stitch, a bobble is formed by increasing and then quickly decreasing a group of stitches. Two sizes of bobbles are used in this book, comprising either five or three stitches, and both are started on WS rows.

MB5 (make 5-st bobble)

1 Work (k1, yo, k1, yo, k1) into the next stitch, making five stitches from one stitch.

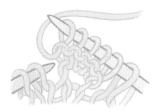

2 Turn, p5, turn, k5, turn, p5. With the five bobble stitches on the right needle, lift the second, third, fourth and fifth stitches over the first stitch and off the right needle. With yarn in front, slip the remaining bobble stitch on to the left needle. Pushing the bobble to the RS of the work if necessary, turn and continue the row.

MB3 (make 3-st bobble)

Work (k1, p1, k1) into the next stitch, making three stitches from one stitch. Turn, p3, turn, k3. Lift the second and third stitches over the first stitch and off the right needle. Push the bobble to the RS of the work if necessary and continue the row.

Bobble Beauty (page 62) features 5-st bobbles.

Catherine Wheel (page 63) features 3-st bobbles.

I-CORD

Perfect for sunflower stems, this round cord is made using two double-pointed needles (dpn). Cast on the specified number of stitches and knit one row in the usual way. The stitches are now on the right needle. *Do not turn, but instead slide the stitches to the other end of the right needle. Transfer this needle with the stitches to your left hand, carry the yarn tightly across the WS of the work and use the empty needle to knit the next row.* Repeat from * to * for length required, then cast off.

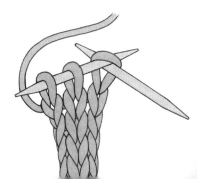

NOTES ON CROCHET

Here is a list of the crochet abbreviations and chart symbols used in this book, plus reminders of some of the key techniques used in the patterns.

ABBREVIATIONS

beg	begin(ning)		**sl st**	slip stitch
ch	chain		**st(s)**	stitch(es)
dc	double crochet		**tog**	together
dtr	double treble crochet		**tr**	treble crochet
htr	half treble crochet		**ttr**	triple treble crochet
MB	make bobble from stitches specified – eg: M5trB = make bobble from 5 treble crochet stitches (see page 21)		**WS**	wrong side of work
			*	asterisks mark a section of instructions to be repeated
rem	remain(ing)		( )	round brackets indicate a group of stitches to be worked together
rep	repeat			
RS	right side of work		[ ]	work instructions in square brackets the number of times stated after the brackets
sk	skip			

CHART SYMBOLS

⊖	slip ring	⌒	work stitch(es) indicated above convex curve in back loop only of stitch below
⊖	chain	▷	starting point/join new colour
•	slip stitch	◁	fasten off
+	double crochet	⟍	start next round/continue at position indicated
⨏	work double crochet in stitch indicated by curved extension	→	direction of working
✕✕	work 2 double crochet together to decrease by 1 stitch (see page 20)	⬤	make 4-tr bobble (see page 21)
T	half treble crochet	◯	make 5-tr bobble (see page 21)
⊤	treble crochet	◯	make 5-dtr bobble (see page 21)
⊤	double treble crochet		
⊤	triple treble crochet		make 6-dtr bobble in back loops of 2 sts below and close bobble with ch 1 (see page 21)
∪	work stitch(es) indicated above concave curve in front loop only of stitch below		

Note: Any symbols joined or grouped together at base should be worked into same stitch below

READING CHARTS

Each crochet design in chapter 3 is accompanied by a chart that should be read with the written instructions. The chart represents the right side of the work.

Charts in rows

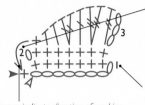

Read rows that are numbered on the left (usually WS rows) from left to right.

Read rows that are numbered on the right (usually RS rows) from right to left.

Arrows indicate direction of working where necessary for clarity, or when it differs from the norm.

Charts in rounds

Charts for working in the round begin at the centre and are read anticlockwise (in the same direction as working) unless stated otherwise.

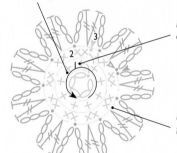

Each round is numbered close to where it begins.

Rounds are separated by pale grey circles for clarity.

CHARTS FOR 3D FLOWERS

Some of the sunflowers have centre discs that can be stuffed to make a three-dimensional flower. These discs are worked as a single piece, increasing outwards from the centre front and then decreasing inwards to the centre back. Where possible, these discs are shown in the form of a single chart. However, for reasons of clarity and space, a few of the larger ones have been drawn as two separate charts – front and back. Read the front chart anticlockwise in the usual way, but read the back chart clockwise (to visualise why this is the case, hold an apple with the stalk at centre front and draw an anticlockwise spiral around it; continue the spiral around to the back of the apple, where you will see that it runs clockwise). The outer round of the front chart is repeated (in a paler colour) as the outer round of the back chart. This is so that you can see clearly where the stitches of the subsequent round should be worked. Do not work this round twice.

FOUNDATION CHAIN

Most pieces of crochet begin with a foundation chain. Start by making a slipknot in the same way as for knitting (see page 13). The slipknot forms the first loop of the foundation chain.

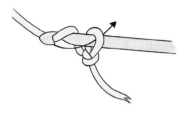

1 Hold the slipknot between the thumb and forefinger of your left hand. Take the yarn over the second finger of the hand so that it is held taut. Take it around the little finger as well if necessary. Your right hand is then free to manipulate the hook. With a turn of the wrist, guide the tip of the hook under the yarn. Catch the yarn and pull it through the loop on the hook to make a chain.

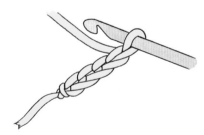

2 Repeat this hooking and catching action to make the number of chains required, moving your left hand every few stitches to hold the foundation chain just below the hook. The same hooking and catching action is used, in various combinations, to form all other crochet stitches.

WORKING IN ROWS

Crochet may be worked back and forth in rows.

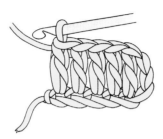

1 Using a foundation chain as the base, with the specified number of chains nearest the hook forming the first stitch, work a stitch into each subsequent chain from right to left. The illustration shows a first row of treble crochet, with three chains forming the first stitch.

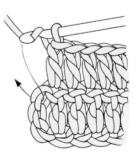

3 The last stitch of this row is worked into the top chain of the three chains that formed the first stitch on the previous row.

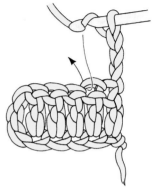

2 Turn the work and make the specified number of chains to form the first stitch of the next row (here, three chains). Be careful to work the second stitch in the right place, as instructed in the pattern. In this example, the second stitch is worked into the second stitch on the previous row. However, if the second stitch was worked into the stitch immediately below instead (that is, into the first stitch on the previous row), this would be the equivalent of making two stitches in the same stitch on the previous row and result in an increase.

Note: Crochet stitches are not symmetrical, as the chain that forms the top of the stitch lies to one side of the main part of the stitch (as can be seen in these illustrations of rows of treble crochet). Beginners may find this disconcerting when first working in rows. Rounds are easier to understand because the stitches all lie in the same direction, usually on the RS of the work.

The centre disc of Aztec Gold (page 91) is worked in rounds and the petals are worked in rows.

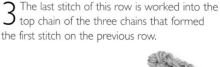

WORKING IN ROUNDS

Pieces worked in the round begin at the centre with either a chain ring or a slip ring, and are then worked outwards in an anticlockwise direction without turning the work at the end of each round. You can substitute a chain ring with a slip ring when making any of the circular pieces in this book, and vice versa.

Chain ring

This method leaves a small hole at the centre, the size depending on the number of chains in the ring.

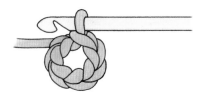

1 Work the required number of chains, then join with a slip stitch in the first chain to form a ring.

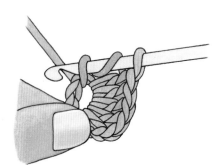

2 Work the first round of stitches around the chain and into the centre of the ring (not into the individual chains). You can work over the starting yarn end at the same time to enclose it. When the first round is complete, gently pull on the starting yarn end to tighten the centre of the chain ring and then trim off the excess.

Slip ring

Also known as a fingerwrap, this method produces a tightly closed centre, leaving no hole unless a large number of stitches is worked on the first round.

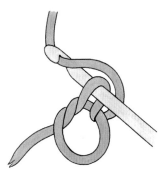

1 Coil the yarn around two fingers and use the hook to pull through a loop of the ball end of the yarn. Do not pull the yarn tight. Holding the ring flat between the thumb and forefinger of your left hand, catch the yarn again and pull it through the loop on the hook to anchor it.

2 Work the first round into the slip ring, working over the starting yarn end at the same time to enclose it. When the first round is complete, gently pull the starting yarn end to close the centre of the slip ring and then trim off the excess.

Concentric rounds or spirals

When crocheting in the round, you can either work in concentric rounds or in a spiral. For concentric rounds, join the last stitch of each round to the first stitch of the round with a slip stitch (pictured). For a spiral, omit the final slip stitch and work continuously so that the lines of stitches spiral outwards. In both cases, you may find it helpful to use a marker to indicate the beginning/end of rounds. Take care to remove and replace the marker on every new round.

Openwork Star (page 84) is worked in spiralling rounds, starting with a chain ring.

JOINING IN A NEW YARN

There are several methods you can use to join in a new yarn or colour.

Using slip stitch

This method can be used when working any stitch. Make a slipknot in the new yarn and place it on the hook. Insert the hook into the work at the specified position and make a slip stitch with the new yarn through both stitch and slipknot. Continue working the pattern with the new yarn.

TIP

When a pattern tells you to join a new yarn with a slip stitch to any stitch on the previous row or round, it is a good idea to join the new yarn to a stitch well away from the yarn end of the previous colour. This avoids having a bunch of yarn ends all in the same place, and makes it easier to enclose the ends neatly on the next row or round, or to weave them in later.

Changing colours mid-stitch

To switch neatly from an old colour to a new colour in the same place, you can leave the last stitch in the old colour incomplete and use the new colour to finish the stitch.

1 Using the old colour, leave the last stage of the final stitch incomplete, so that there are two loops on the hook. Wrap the new colour over the hook and pull it through the loops on the hook to complete the stitch.

2 Continue working with the new colour. You may find it easier to knot the two loose ends together before you cut the yarn no longer in use, leaving ends of about 10cm (4in). Always undo the knot before weaving in the yarn ends.

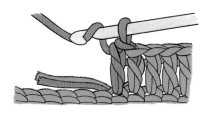

WORK 2 DC TOGETHER (dc2tog)

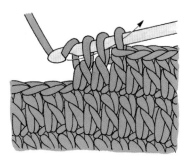

Decrease one double crochet stitch by working two stitches together. Insert the hook into the first stitch, wrap the yarn over the hook and draw through, leaving two loops on the hook. Repeat in the next stitch, leaving three loops on the hook. Wrap the yarn over the hook again and draw through all three loops to finish the decrease.

FRONT AND BACK LOOPS

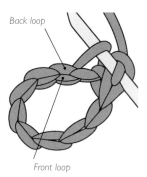

Back loop

Front loop

Each crochet stitch has two strands of yarn that form the top of the stitch – the front and back loops. Unless instructed otherwise, always insert the hook under both of these loops when working subsequent stitches. The technique of working into just the front loop or the back loop is used in this book to work multiple layers of petals in the same place.

BOBBLES

A bobble is a group of stitches worked into the same stitch at the base and joined together at the top.

M5trB (make 5-tr bobble)

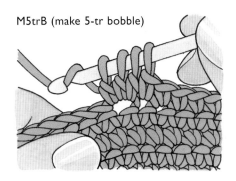
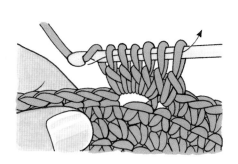
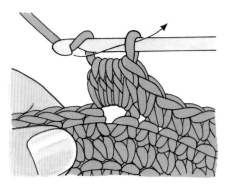

1 Wrap the yarn over the hook and work the first treble crochet, omitting the last stage of the stitch to leave two loops on the hook. Work the second and third tr in the same way and in the same place. You now have four loops on the hook.

2 Work the fourth and fifth tr of the bobble as before, resulting in six loops on the hook in total. Wrap the yarn over the hook and draw it through all six loops to secure them.

3 Work a chain stitch to complete the bobble, pushing the bobble through to the RS with the tip of a finger as you draw the chain through.

M4trB (make 4-tr bobble)

Work as for 5-tr bobble but only work 4 tr, leaving five loops on the hook in total. Complete the bobble in the usual way with a securing loop and a final chain stitch.

M5dtrB (make 5-dtr bobble)

Work as for 5-tr bobble but work double treble rather than treble crochet stitches.

M6dtrB (make 6-dtr bobble)

The 6-dtr bobble featured in this book varies from all the other bobbles in that the base of the bobble is worked into the back loops of two stitches rather than into a single stitch. Work the first 3 dtr in the usual way into the back loop of the first stitch (four loops on hook); work the remaining 3 dtr in the usual way in the back loop of the second stitch (seven loops on hook in total). Complete the bobble in the usual way with a securing loop and a final chain stitch.

Autumn Beauty (page 90) features three rounds of 5-tr bobbles.

Purple Passion (page 82) combines 4-tr (pink) and 5-dtr (orange) bobbles.

Large Bud (page 85) features 6-dtr bobbles around the outer edge.

ADDITIONAL KNOW-HOW

All of the sunflowers and other designs in this book are easy to assemble using just a few standard finishing techniques. Here are some tips and suggestions.

SEWING SEAMS AND WEAVING IN YARN ENDS

Here are a few guidelines for successful assembly:
• When making any flower or project, read through the pattern first and think ahead, leaving a long end of yarn where it will be useful for sewing a seam.
• When ends of yarn will not be used for seaming, you may be able to enclose some of them while working the piece. If not, the ends should be woven in on the wrong side after completion.
• Yarn ends left at the tips of petals or leaves may be easier to weave in before the main flower assembly.
• Use a yarn or tapestry needle to weave in ends, and always weave in for at least 5cm (2in) to prevent the end from slipping out again. For smooth, slippery yarns, reverse the direction and weave back again for a few stitches. Trim off the excess.
• If a new length of yarn needs to be joined for seaming, use matching yarn and start with a couple of small backstitches rather than a knot because a knot can easily slip through to the right side of the piece.
• Take care to sew all seams firmly, especially when making items for children.

Use a yarn or tapestry needle to weave in yarn ends on the wrong side.

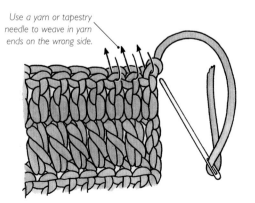

STUFFING

The centre discs of the three-dimensional flowers in this book are shaped by stuffing. Leftover matching yarn makes ideal stuffing because there will be no show-through – this is especially useful for crochet flowers where the stitch structure is looser than on knitted flowers. Either stuff with cut-up pieces of yarn or wind off short lengths of yarn and push these in, one coil at a time.

Alternatively, you can use synthetic toy stuffing, such as polyester fibre filling. Push the stuffing in firmly, one wisp at a time, using it to shape the item without distorting it. Too much stuffing will pack down, whereas too little will never plump up.

Polyester fibre filling is useful for stuffing large flowers like Woolly Mammoth (page 58).

Save leftover yarn to use as stuffing.

BLOCKING

Blocking is used to 'set' the shape of knit and crochet pieces and to even out uneven stitches for a professional finish. Be aware that blocking will flatten out the pieces, especially petals and leaves, so the decision of whether to block or not really depends on what you want the finished flower (or other item) to look like – it is entirely up to you. You can block individual pieces separately or after sewing together.

To block a piece of knit or crochet, ease and pin the piece into shape on a well-padded surface, then either steam with an iron or spray with cold water, depending on the fibre content of the yarn. Alternatively, the piece can be hand-washed in lukewarm water before pinning out. Always be guided by the care information given on the ball band of the yarn because most synthetic fibres are easily damaged by heat. When in doubt, choose the cold-water method for blocking synthetic fibres. Allow the piece to dry completely before unpinning.

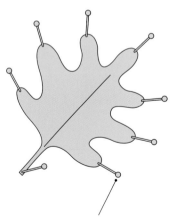

Glass-headed pins have large heads and are the best type to use for blocking because they are easy to see and will not melt with the application of steam.

The wings of the Honey Bee (page 70) are knitted from fine wire, while the antennae and legs are formed from wire hair grips.

WIRING

To create a feeling of movement in petals and leaves, you may wish to wire them to make them easier to bend and sculpt. You can use craft, jewellery or florist wire, all of which come in a wide range of colours and gauges (thicknesses). Choose a fine wire, such as 0.5mm (24 gauge), and simply pass the wire through the stitches around the outer edges of the petal or leaf; you may find it easier to thread the wire into a yarn needle to do this. Be careful not to leave a burr when snipping the wire, and use pliers to twist and tuck the ends safely away. You can also thread wire through a stem to make it bendable, but see page 112 for adding stronger support to stems for holding them upright in a vase. Wire is also used to create the features of some of the small creatures in this book. However, remember that you should never wire an item that is intended for use by children.

Round-nose pliers are useful for neatening ends of wire.

ANTENNAE

A couple of the small creatures in this book require yarn antennae. Insert the yarn needle at the position of the first antenna, leaving a yarn end. Bring the needle out at the position of the second antenna, backstitch between the two, then bring the yarn out again at the second antenna position. Trim both ends. If desired, you can stiffen the antennae by pinning out straight and spraying with a fabric stiffener or strong hairspray. Allow to dry. Hair grips can also be bent into the shape of antennae and inserted through the knit or crochet piece.

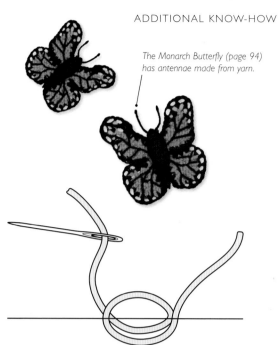

The Monarch Butterfly (page 94) has antennae made from yarn.

POMPOMS

A couple of the flowers in this book require pompoms. Either use a ready-made plastic pompom maker or cut out two rings of cardboard.

1 Place the two rings together and use a yarn needle to wrap yarn around them.

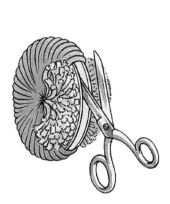

2 Starting new lengths of yarn at the outside edge, continue until the rings are tightly covered. Insert the blade of a pair of scissors between the rings and cut the yarn around the edge.

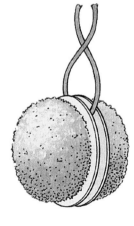

3 Tie a length of yarn around the pompom between the rings. Knot the yarn tightly, slip the rings off and trim the pompom. Use the ends of yarn from the tie for attaching the pompom to the flower.

FELTING

When woollen knitting or crochet is washed vigorously in hot water and then rinsed in cold water, the fibres mat together and the knitting or crochet shrinks to form a sturdy, dense fabric.

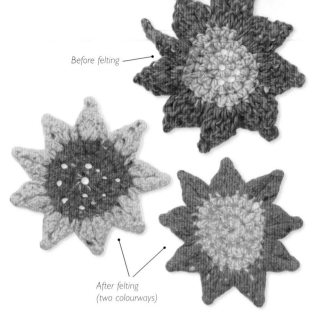

Before felting

After felting
(two colourways)

Picot Star (page 75) before and after felting. Note the amount of shrinkage and how the colours fade slightly and the stitches blend together in the fuzzy surface of the felt.

HOW DOES IT WORK?

Why does sheep's wool and other animal fibres felt? Each tiny fibre is covered with little scales. When the fibre is subjected to friction and an abrupt change in temperature, the little scales lock upon each other and shrink together, causing the individual fibres to become matted and permanently entangled. It is not possible to reverse the felting process. Once wool is felted, it is felted for good. Luckily, the dense fabric created by felting is fabulous for all kinds of sculptural treatments, including sunflowers and leaves.

Pure wool yarn is the best choice for felting.

CHOOSING YARNS

Here are some guidelines for choosing a yarn that will shrink and felt successfully:

• Choose a yarn that is made of at least 80 per cent animal fibre. This includes fibres from sheep (wool), alpaca, llama, angora rabbits and goats (mohair).

• Pure wool yarn is the best choice – it should shrink by 25 per cent or more in the felting process. Wool/synthetic blends may shrink to a lesser degree. Vegetable fibres such as cotton hardly shrink at all. Silk from silkworms will not felt.

• Yarns labelled 'superwash' or 'machine washable' have been specially treated to resist shrinkage and will therefore not felt satisfactorily, even if they are 100 per cent wool.

• Be aware that different yarns will felt differently and in varying numbers of wash cycles. Single-ply loosely spun wools, for example, will felt in one cycle to produce a dense, fuzzy fabric in which the original stitches are almost indistinguishable. Yarns that are more tightly spun, on the other hand, tend to retain more of the appearance of the knit or crochet stitches, and may take three or four wash cycles to felt adequately.

• Take care when choosing colours, because some of the dye may be washed out during the felting process.

MACHINE FELTING

Felting by machine is easier than by hand but is very much a case of trial and error, because each washing machine varies.

1 Collect all the little pieces and put them into a zip-up net lingerie bag (or similar). This is not essential, but it will help to keep the little bits of petals, flowers, leaves and stems together in one place.

2 Put the bag into the washing machine and add some other items to the load, such as an old pair of jeans or some bed sheets, for added friction. If you have a couple of old tennis balls, throw them in too. Avoid putting terrycloth towels in the load because they can shed and the fibres will become permanently embedded in your flowers.

3 Set the washing machine to a hot wash and cold rinse. Add some laundry detergent and let the cycle run. If you have a machine that can be stopped during the cycle, you can check on the progress of the felting and remove the items when they have shrunk the required amount. Otherwise, just let the cycle run until

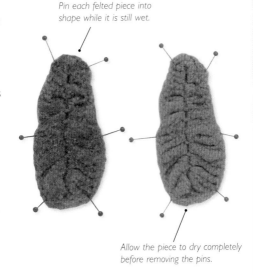

Pin each felted piece into shape while it is still wet.

Allow the piece to dry completely before removing the pins.

it is complete, then remove your project and examine. If the individual stitches are still visible, run it through another cycle to felt it further.

4 Once you are happy with the degree of felting (a matter of personal taste), you will need to neaten the pieces. Rinse well in clean water, squeezing out as much excess water as you can. Pin the pieces out to shape on a rug or a corkboard; for small felted pieces, you can use the glass-headed pins you would use for blocking (page 22), but large T-pins can be useful for holding larger and thicker felted pieces in place. If the pieces are completely distorted, use a hot iron to help flatten them. Allow them to dry completely.

TIP

If you really get into felting, purchase a used washing machine and keep it only for your felting projects. Felting a lot of wool can add extra wear and tear on a washing machine and shorten its life.

HAND FELTING

It is possible to felt by hand, though it will take longer and entail more physical work than machine felting.

1 Prepare a bowl of hot, soapy water and another of very cold water. Immerse the knit or crochet piece in the hot water and allow to soak for a few minutes.

2 Lift the piece out of the water and rub it vigorously between your hands or, better still, on something such as a washboard. Continue until the piece begins to shrink.

3 Brush the surface gently with a nailbrush to fluff up the fibres, then plunge the piece into the cold water. Repeat the hot/rub/cold process several times if required.

Use a nailbrush to fluff up the fibres of the felted fabric.

4 Rinse thoroughly in fresh cold water, squeeze out the excess moisture and leave flat to dry, pinning into shape if necessary.

EMBELLISHMENT

While the sunflowers and other designs in this book are perfectly fine left undecorated, it can be fun to add extra special details, such as embroidery and beads.

The petals of Lazy Daisy (page 61) are embellished with large lazy daisy stitches.

The wings of the Swallowtail Butterfly (page 68) are embroidered with running stitch.

French knots are worked around the centre disc of this felted Raspberry Ruffle (page 78).

EMBROIDERY STITCHES

There is a huge variety of decorative embroidery stitches to choose from. A few very simple ones are demonstrated here, but feel free to experiment with any other embroidery stitches you may already know. To make the stitches really stand out, use a double strand of yarn or thread to work them.

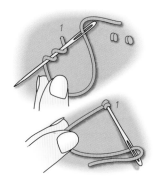

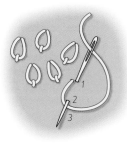

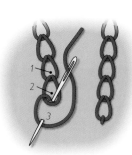

Running stitch
To work a line of running stitch, bring the needle up at 1, down at 2 and up again at 3. Continue in this way for length required.

French knot
Bring the needle up at 1 and wind the thread twice around the needle tip (top). Holding the thread, insert the needle very close to – but not exactly at – 1 and pull through gently (bottom).

Lazy daisy stitch
This is also known as single chain stitch. Bring the needle up at 1, form a loop with the thread and insert the needle again at 1. Bring the needle up at 2, inside the loop, and pull through. Insert the needle at 3, catching down the loop of thread.

Chain stitch
This is worked in the same way as a lazy daisy (single chain) stitch, but point 3 is moved a bit farther away from point 2. Work as many chain stitches as required, then finish with a little stitch to hold the last loop in place.

Experiment with different fibres, such as shiny perle cotton embroidery thread. Use multiple strands to achieve the thickness of thread you require.

Beads are available in a huge range of materials, from colourful plastic to shiny metal.

BEADS

Sewing beads on to a flower (or other design) is an easy way to add textural interest. There are literally thousands of different styles of beads now available at your local craft shop. Look for wooden beads to add a rustic feeling to a sunflower. Children's plastic craft beads are easy to attach and can add a pop of colour to a project. Shiny and metallic beads will dress up a sunflower to make it an accessory worthy of a night on the town on a little black dress.

Beads can be attached randomly, or you can create a pattern by following any lines of shaping worked in the centre discs of the flowers. For a really colourful effect, sew different colours of beads all over the centre of the flower. Take care not to attach beads to a flower intended for a small child because of the possibility of the child swallowing the bead.

EMBROIDERY THREADS

Although embroidery is traditionally worked with thin thread, heavier knit and crochet yarns have been used to work the embroidery in this book. If using traditional stranded embroidery thread, combine several strands to make the weight of thread you need for the effect you wish to achieve.

Dig into your yarn stash to add embroidery to the flowers. Try experimenting with yarns and threads in different textures and fibres. A mercerised cotton will add a bit of shine, while a metallic yarn will lend a touch of glamour. Space-dyed and variegated (multicolour) yarns are fun to embroider with, too. Ribbon can also be used for embroidery, although it will be difficult to pull ribbon through felted flowers.

EMBROIDERY TIPS

• To begin and end embroidery, take a couple of small stitches on the back of the flower (or other design) to anchor the thread, leaving a 1.3cm (1/2in) end of thread. Knots can pop through to the front of the work.
• Don't pull the embroidery thread too tight. The flowers are stretchy and you want them to remain so.
• If you plan to felt your sunflower, work the embroidery after felting is complete.
• Use a blunt-ended needle with a large eye (such as a tapestry needle) for embroidery on non-felted flowers. On felted flowers, use a needle with a large eye and a sharp point.

BEADING TIPS

• Use a sewing needle and durable sewing thread to attach beads. Stranded embroidery thread is ideal because it can be split into strands and recombined to a thickness suitable for both fabric and embellishment.
• Choose a thread colour that will match the base colour of the flower where the beads will be attached.
• Begin by taking a couple of small stitches on the back of the flower to anchor the thread. Bring the needle to the front and pass it through the bead. Take the needle to the back again and make a couple of small stitches to finish off.
• When carrying the thread across the back of the flower, make sure not to pull the thread too tight or it will cause the flower to pucker. Leave the thread too loose, however, and the bead will hang droopy and may snag.

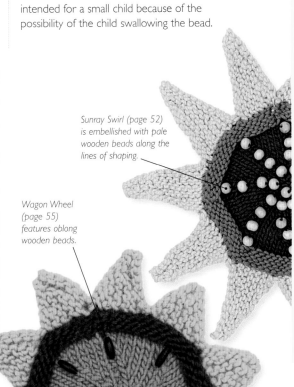

Sunray Swirl (page 52) is embellished with pale wooden beads along the lines of shaping.

Wagon Wheel (page 55) features oblong wooden beads.

ALL ABOUT COLOUR

Many knitters and crocheters lack confidence when combining colours, but working with colour is fun and addictive once you understand the way colours work together.

COLOUR WHEEL

Some people seem to have more of an aptitude for colour than others, but it is possible to learn how to use colour to great effect by exploring the basic principles of colour theory. Always remember, however, that colour is a personal choice – there are no hard-and-fast rules.

Designers in many fields use the colour wheel to help them choose colour schemes. When you were a child, you learned to draw a rainbow – Mother Nature's ultimate colour show – and a colour wheel is simply a 'rainbow in the round'.

The colour wheel is made of three primary colours (1): red, blue and yellow. These are mixed in pairs to create the secondary colours (2): violet, green and orange. These in turn are mixed with their neighbours to create tertiary colours (3).

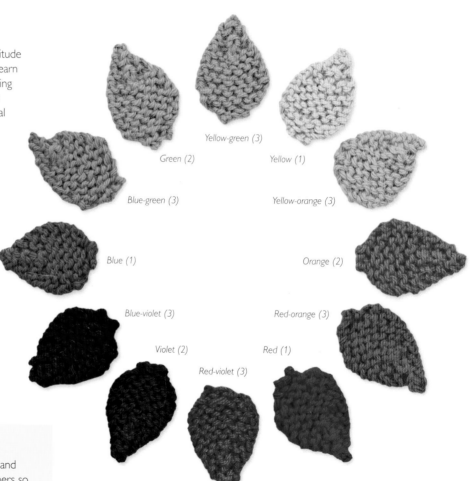

Yellow-green (3)

Green (2)

Yellow (1)

Blue-green (3)

Yellow-orange (3)

Blue (1)

Orange (2)

Blue-violet (3)

Red-orange (3)

Violet (2)

Red (1)

Red-violet (3)

A colour wheel made from sunflower petals. You could use yarns from your yarn stash to make a host of colourful sunflower petals and then mix and match them to try out different colour combinations.

TIP

Separate your yarns into colour groups and keep these in transparent plastic containers so that you have ready-made palettes of colour to work with. Don't limit yourself to knitting yarn; try looking for interesting colours among embroidery threads as well.

HARMONIOUS COLOURS

Colours that are next to each other on the colour wheel (such as blue, blue-green and green) are called harmonious or analogous colours. These colours are closely related in tone and feel harmonious and peaceful. Harmonious colours can be used to enhance one another.

COMPLEMENTARY COLOURS

Colours that are opposite each other on the colour wheel (such as green and red) are called complementary colours. Used together, complementary colours create vibrant, contrasting combinations. When using a complementary colour combination, the human response is to be stimulated and happy. Although you may not want to walk around every day wearing complementary colour combinations, it is fun to use them sparingly in your wardrobe and in your home. By adding just a little bit of a colour's complement to a project, it will make the project have more life and pizzazz. Try choosing slightly softened shades for a rich, rather than clashing, result.

An example of harmonious colours in nature would be a sunflower with shades of yellow-green, yellow and yellow-orange.

This photograph of a bunch of yellow and orange sunflowers with just a little bit of blue sky in the background illustrates how a complementary colour (blue) can make the other colours more interesting and vibrant.

A warm yellow and yellow-orange sunflower viewed against a cool blue sky is an example of a complementary colour combination in nature.

COLOUR TEMPERATURE

The colour wheel is also divided into warm and cool colours. The colours on the orange side of the wheel, from yellow to red-violet, are known as warm colours. These have a glowing intensity that needs careful management. Choose them for bright, cheerful impact. The colours on the blue side of the wheel, from violet to yellow-green, are known as cool colours. Used together, these tend to give a more restful and calming effect.

An infinite number of colour mixes creates a vast array of shades within these two basic colour groups. So a yellow that contains a certain amount of orange is called a warm yellow, while a greenish yellow is a cool yellow. Similarly, a reddish violet would be warm, while a bluish violet would be cool. Combining warm and cool colours can create useful optical illusions, with warm colours appearing to advance and cool colours appearing to recede.

Cool colour yarns

Warm colour yarns

NEUTRALS

Neutral colours, such as cream and brown, do not appear as pure colours on the colour wheel. Artists make neutrals by mixing pigments together – for example, mixing colours opposite each other on the wheel to produce a range of muted greys and soft browns. Neutrals, therefore, work well with all colours on the colour wheel and can be used to great effect to set off other colours – just as the brown seedhead of a sunflower is the perfect foil for any petal colour.

Complementary (opposite) colours on the colour wheel are a vibrant combination that can be softened with the addition of a neutral colour.

COLOUR VALUE

Learning how to play with colour value is the next step in working successfully with colour in your knitting and crochet. Value is the lightness or darkness of a colour. There are dark colours and light colours within each particular shade on the colour wheel. If you make a project in colours that are all the same value, the different parts of the project will not stand out from each other. This can be seen in nature, too. A single-colour yellow sunflower is beautiful, but it will appear as a plain yellow circle from a distance. A sunflower with yellow petals and a deep orange centre, on the other hand, will still look distinctively like a flower from far away because of its darker centre. As with colour temperature, light colours appear to come forwards and dark colours to recede.

The colours of the petals and seedhead of this sunflower are very close in value, so the individual parts of the flower do not stand out very strongly from one another.

A classic sunflower with yellow petals and a dark orange-brown centre is an example of different colour values. This is nature playing dark against light. The warm colours of the flowers also appear to pop forwards from the background of cool green foliage.

The darker colour value of the centre disc of Starfish (page 92) combined with the lighter colour value of the petals helps to define the shape of the sunflower in imitation of the classic sunflower colour combination found in nature.

The bright gold centre disc of Little Gem (page 75) appears to pop forwards from its frame of neutral brown petals.

Collect some leaves and observe how the colours of the colour wheel are combined in nature.

NATURAL INSPIRATION

If you get stuck when trying to choose colours, simply take a walk and observe how Mother Nature does it – she is the best teacher. Look closely at how colours are combined in nature. Pick up a leaf and identify the different shades that are actually in the leaf. A leaf is not only green – it is green, red, blue and yellow. Once you make it a priority to start really observing how colours are put together in nature, you will realise that putting them together yourself is not that hard. Now bring the leaf inside, pull out your yarn stash and begin arranging matching colours of yarn next to the leaf. Try making a test strip or small swatch, a leaf or a flower using the yarns – this is your first step to increasing your familiarity with colour.

TIME TO EXPERIMENT

You can spend your entire life learning about colours and how they all work together, but the important thing is to start putting the theory into practice and experimenting. All of the sunflowers in this book are perfect for gaining confidence when working with colour. They are small and quick to make. Treat each one that you make as a chance to experiment with all of the colours that you have in your yarn stash. Go ahead – make a yellow sunflower with a blue centre, or make a red sunflower with a chartreuse (yellow-green) centre. Play with different colour combinations and see what happens. You will learn something new every time you create a new flower. You will be off on your own colour adventure.

Openwork Star (page 84)

Catherine Wheel (page 63)

Match yarns from your yarn stash to the colours in the leaves.

Whether using harmonious or complementary colours, a useful trick for adding definition and vibrancy to your sunflowers is to use a contrasting colour to separate the petals and centre disc.

Amethyst Queen (page 63)

DIRECTORY

This chapter showcases a stunning collection of knit and crochet sunflowers, leaves, stems and small creatures. Look through the directory to help you choose the design you want to make. Each design is labelled with a number that corresponds to a pattern in the instructions chapter (pages 50–95), so once you have selected your design, turn to the relevant page and begin.

22 I-CORD STEM

26 VEINED LEAVES

50 LACE SUNBEAM

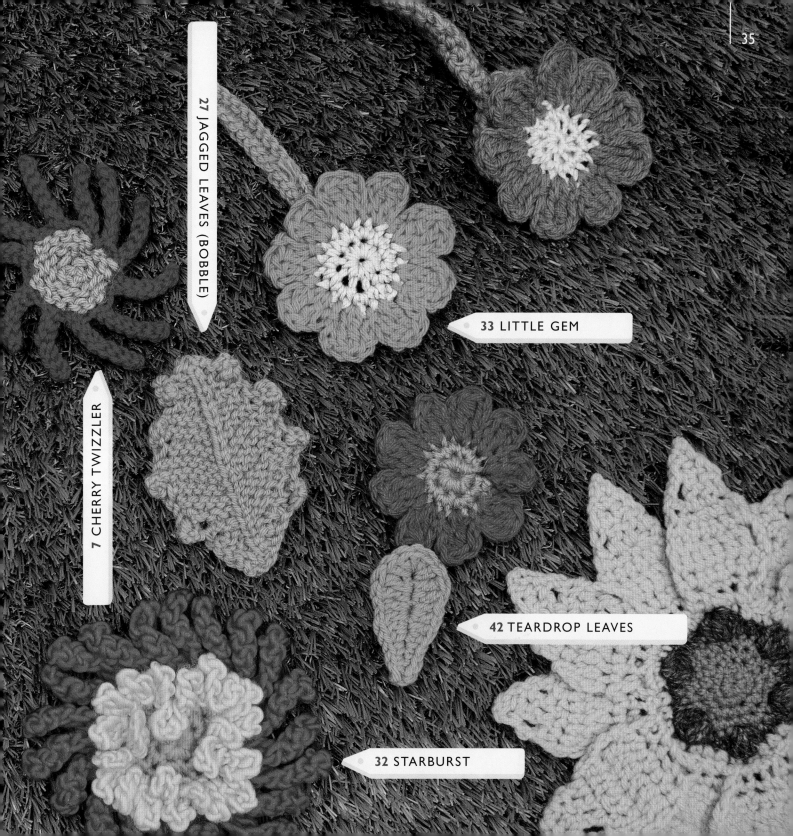

27 JAGGED LEAVES (BOBBLE)

33 LITTLE GEM

7 CHERRY TWIZZLER

42 TEARDROP LEAVES

32 STARBURST

8 COCOA SUNDROP

34 PICOT STAR

52 AUTUMN BEAUTY

42 TEARDROP LEAVES

42 TOOTHED LEAVES

3 SMALL TEDDY BEAR

19 POMPOM GEM (FELTED)

41 CROCHET PETALS

19 POMPOM GEM

6 WAGON WHEEL

10 JOKER

42 TEARDROP LEAVES

11 TOFFEE TWIST

53 AZTEC GOLD

26 VEINED LEAVES

51 BICOLOUR GEM

12 WOOLLY MAMMOTH

36 BIG TEDDY BEAR

34 PICOT STAR (FELTED)

30 WOOLLY BEAR CATERPILLAR

25 VEINED PETALS

37 RASPBERRY RUFFLE (FELTED)

49 TWEED GIANT

9 POMPOM PUFF

47 SMALL BUD

48 LARGE BUD

27 JAGGED LEAVES (BOBBLE)

55 LADYBIRD

1 SUNRAY SWIRL

7 FIRECRACKER

16 SWEET PETITE

18 BOBBLE BEAUTY

42 TEARDROP LEAVES

43 PURPLE PASSION

29 HONEY BEE

33 LITTLE GEM (FELTED)

37 RASPBERRY RUFFLE

43 & 40 PURPLE PASSION WITH FLOWER BACK AND STEM

34 PICOT STAR

26 VEINED LEAVES

37 RASPBERRY RUFFLE (CURLED)

28 SWALLOWTAIL BUTTERFLY

20 AMETHYST QUEEN

5 GIANT SUNGOLD

45 OPENWORK STAR

42 TEARDROP LEAVES

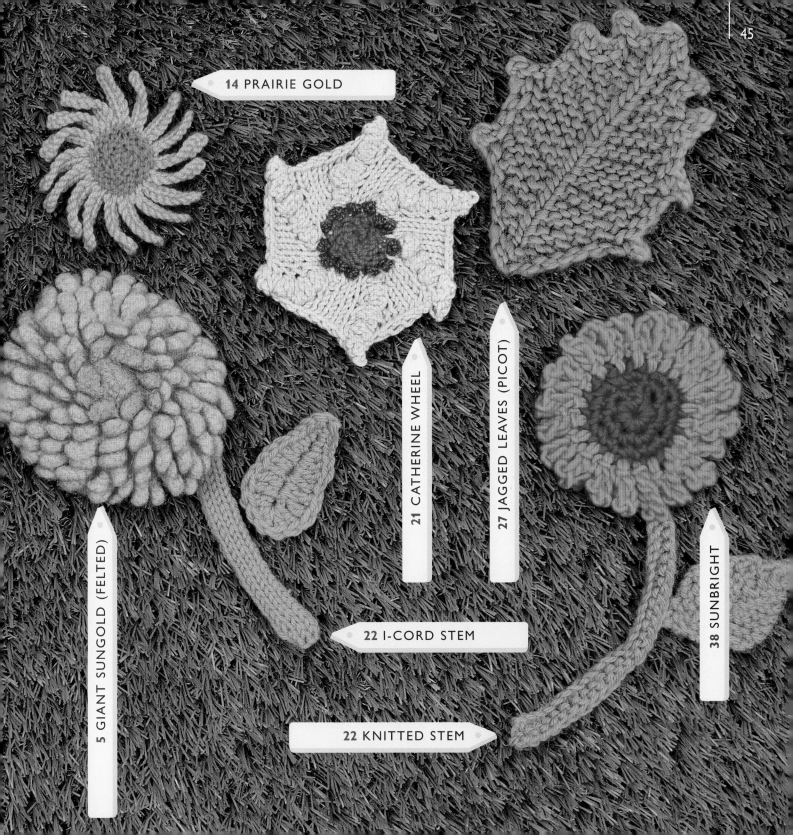

14 PRAIRIE GOLD

21 CATHERINE WHEEL

27 JAGGED LEAVES (PICOT)

5 GIANT SUNGOLD (FELTED)

22 I-CORD STEM

38 SUNBRIGHT

22 KNITTED STEM

39 SUNBURST

42 TEARDROP LEAVES

SAPRICOT STAR (FELTED)

171 LAZY DAISY

46 SEA ANEMONE

49 TWEED GIANT

4 CRÈME CARAMEL

23 KNITTED STEM

31 ROBIN

42 TOOTHED LEAVES

40 CROCHET STEM

41 CROCHET PETALS

54 STARFISH (FELTED)

44 RUBY HARVEST

13 SWIZZLE STICKS

35 MOULIN ROUGE

42 TOOTHED LEAVES

56 MONARCH BUTTERFLY

54 STARFISH

23 GARTER PETALS

15 GOLD STRIPE

42 TEARDROP LEAVES

24 CONCAVE PETALS

22 KNITTED STEM

INSTRUCTIONS

Organised into knitting and crochet, this chapter contains instructions on how to create all of the designs featured in the directory (pages 32–49). For the crochet designs, charts are provided to be used in conjunction with the written instructions.

KNITTED DESIGNS

Sunray Swirl
directory view page 41

Yarn: Aran-weight cotton in yellow (A), green (B) and dark brown (C)

Extras: Thirty-three 6mm (¼in) round pale wooden beads; brown sewing thread and needle

Size: Approx. 24cm (9½in) diameter, using 4.5mm needles

METHOD

PETALS (make 11)

Using A, cast on 13 sts.

*Row 1: Knit.

Place marker at beginning of next row to indicate start of short-row shaping.

Row 2: K4, turn.

Row 3: K4 to end.

Row 4: K8, turn.

Row 5: K8 to end.

Row 6: K11, turn.

Row 7: K11 to end.

Rows 8–9: As rows 4–5.

Rows 10–11: As rows 2–3.

Row 12: K13 to end.

Cast off 12 sts to complete first petal.

Slip remaining stitch on to left needle and cast on 12 sts using knitted cast-on technique. (13 sts)*

Rep from * to * to make strip of 11 petals in total, casting off all 13 sts to complete the last petal. Either side of strip may be used as RS.

CENTRE DISC

Hold petal strip with unattached ends of petals hanging down. Using B and with RS facing, pick up and knit 7 sts from base of each petal along top edge of strip. (77 sts)

Row 1 (WS): [K2tog, k13] 5 times, k2. (72 sts)

Row 2: Purl.

Row 3: Knit.

Row 4: [P2tog, p7] 8 times. (64 sts) Break off B and join C.

Row 5 & all WS rows: Purl.

Row 6: [Ssk, k6] 8 times. (56 sts)

Row 8: [Ssk, k5] 8 times. (48 sts)

Row 10: [Ssk, k4] 8 times. (40 sts)

Row 12: [Ssk, k3] 8 times. (32 sts)

Row 14: [Ssk, k2] 8 times. (24 sts)

Row 16: [Ssk, k1] 8 times. (16 sts)

Row 18: [Ssk] 8 times. (8 sts)

Row 19: Purl.

Break off yarn, leaving 20cm (8in) tail. Thread tail into a yarn needle and pass through remaining 8 sts. Tighten to close centre of disc.

FINISHING

Using tails of yarn, sew side edges of centre disc together to form a circle. Using sewing thread, sew four beads along each yarn C ridge (formed by the decreasing) on centre disc to create a swirling pattern. Sew one bead at centre.

2 *Firecracker*
directory view page 41

Yarn: DK-weight wool in red (A) and chartreuse (B)
Size: Approx. 12.5cm (5in) diameter, using 4mm needles

METHOD
PETALS (make 24)
Using A, cast on 15 sts.
Cast off 14 sts to complete first petal. (1 st remains)
*Slip remaining st on to left needle and cast on 14 sts using knitted cast-on technique. (15 sts)
Cast off 14 sts. (1 st remains)*
Rep from * to * to make strip of 24 petals in total.
Break off yarn, leaving 25cm (10in) tail, and pass through remaining stitch.
Either side of strip may be used as RS.

CENTRE DISC
Using B, cast on 3 sts.
Row 1: Knit.
Row 2: [Kfb] 3 times. (6 sts)
Row 3: Knit.
Row 4: [Kfb] 6 times. (12 sts)
Rows 5–7: Knit.
Row 8: [K2tog] 6 times.
(6 sts)
Row 9: Knit.
Row 10: [K2tog] 3 times.
(3 sts)
Row 11: Knit.
Break off yarn, leaving 20cm (8in) tail. Thread tail into a yarn needle and pass through remaining 3 sts. Tighten to close centre of disc.

FINISHING
Using tail of yarn, sew side edges of centre disc together to form a hollow ball. If desired, stuff loosely with scraps of yarn B (or similar colour) as you sew the side seam. Bring cast-on and cast-off edges together to flatten the ball and stitch tightly through centre. Run yarn tail of petal strip through edge of strip where petals are joined. Use tail to gather up edge to a length that will form a double coil to fit behind centre disc. Secure the double coil with a few stitches through both layers, then sew centre disc in place.

3 *Small Teddy Bear*
directory view page 37

Yarn: DK-weight cotton in green (A) and chartreuse (C); fringed yarn in lemon yellow (B)
Size: Approx. 7cm (2³⁄₄in) diameter, using 4mm needles

METHOD
Begin at centre back as follows:
Using A, cast on 8 sts.
Row 1 (RS): Knit.
Rows 2, 4, 6 & 8: Purl.
Row 3: [Kfb] 8 times. (16 sts)
Row 5: [K1, kfb] 8 times. (24 sts)
Row 7: [K2, kfb] 8 times. (32 sts)
Row 9: [K3, kfb] 8 times. (40 sts)
Row 10: Purl.
Break off A and join B.
Rows 11–14: Knit.
Row 15: [K3, k2tog] 8 times. (32 sts)
Row 16: [K2, k2tog] 8 times. (24 sts)
Row 17: [K1, k2tog] 8 times. (16 sts)
Break off B and join C.
Row 18: Purl.
Row 19: [K2tog] 8 times. (8 sts)
Row 20: Purl.
Break off yarn, leaving 20cm (8in) tail. Thread tail into a yarn needle and pass through remaining 8 sts. Tighten to close centre of flower.

FINISHING
Using tails of yarn, sew side edges together to form a hollow ball, stuffing lightly with scraps of matching yarn if desired. To shape flower centre, stitch firmly through centre point, joining front and back closely together; then stitch firmly all around centre disc of yarn C through both layers of knitting.

Unstuffed felted variation worked in wool yarn with French knot embroidery.

4 Crème Caramel
directory view page 47

Yarn: Aran-weight wool in caramel (A), magenta (B) and chartreuse (C)
Size: Approx. 12.5cm (5in) diameter, using 4.5mm needles

METHOD

PETALS (make 8)
Using A, make eight small garter petals (see page 64).

CENTRE DISC
Using B and with RS facing, pick up and knit 3 sts from base of each petal. (24 sts)
Row 1 (WS): Knit. Break off B and join C.
Row 2: [Ssk, k1] 8 times. (16 sts)
Row 3: Knit.
Row 4: [Ssk] 8 times. (8 sts)
Row 5: [Ssk] 4 times. (4 sts)
Break off yarn, leaving 20cm (8in) tail. Thread tail into a yarn needle and pass through remaining 4 sts. Tighten to close centre of disc, then sew side edges of disc together to form a circle.

5 Giant Sungold
directory view pages 44 & 45

Yarn: Aran-weight wool in golden yellow (A) and green (B)
Size: Approx. 14cm (5¹⁄₂in) diameter, using 4.5mm needles

METHOD

Note: MP = make petal (see page 15).

CENTRE DISC AND PETALS
Using A, cast on 48 sts.
Row 1 (RS): Knit.
Row 2: [K1, MP, k1] 24 times. (24 petals and 48 sts)
Row 3: Knit.
Row 4: [K2, MP] 24 times. (24 petals and 48 sts)
Row 5: [K4, k2tog] 8 times. (40 sts)
Row 6: [K1, MP, k1] 20 times. (20 petals and 40 sts)
Row 7: [K3, k2tog] 8 times. (32 sts)
Row 8: [K2, MP] 16 times. (16 petals and 32 sts)
Row 9: [K2, k2tog] 8 times. (24 sts)
Row 10: [K1, MP, k1] 12 times. (12 petals and 24 sts)
Row 11: [K1, k2tog] 8 times. (16 sts)
From this point on, make smaller petals by casting on and casting off 4 sts (instead of 5).
Row 12: [K2, MP] 8 times. (8 petals and 16 sts) Break off A and join B.
Row 13: [K2tog] 8 times. (8 sts)
Row 14: [K1, MP] 8 times. (8 petals and 8 sts)
Row 15: Knit.
Break off yarn, leaving 20cm (8in) tail. Thread tail into a yarn needle and pass through remaining 8 sts. Tighten to close centre of flower, then sew side edges together to form a circle.

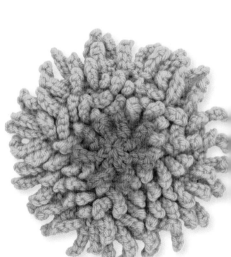

6 Wagon Wheel
directory view page 37

Yarn: Chunky-weight wool in golden yellow (A), brown (B) and orange (C)
Extras: Eight 15mm (5/8in) oblong dark wooden beads; orange sewing thread and needle
Size: Approx. 20cm (8in) diameter, using 5.5mm needles

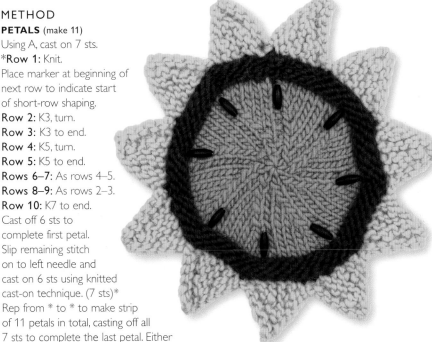

METHOD
PETALS (make 11)
Using A, cast on 7 sts.
*****Row 1:** Knit.
Place marker at beginning of next row to indicate start of short-row shaping.
Row 2: K3, turn.
Row 3: K3 to end.
Row 4: K5, turn.
Row 5: K5 to end.
Rows 6–7: As rows 4–5.
Rows 8–9: As rows 2–3.
Row 10: K7 to end.
Cast off 6 sts to complete first petal.
Slip remaining stitch on to left needle and cast on 6 sts using knitted cast-on technique. (7 sts)*
Rep from * to * to make strip of 11 petals in total, casting off all 7 sts to complete the last petal. Either side of strip may be used as RS.

CENTRE DISC
Hold petal strip with unattached ends of petals hanging down. Using B and with RS facing, pick up and knit 6 sts from base of each petal along top edge of strip. (66 sts)
Row 1 (WS): Knit.
Row 2: Purl.
Row 3: [K2tog, k31] twice. (64 sts)
Break off B and join C.
Row 4: Knit.
Row 5 & all WS rows: Purl.
Row 6: [Ssk, k6] 8 times. (56 sts)
Row 8: [Ssk, k5] 8 times. (48 sts)
Row 10: [Ssk, k4] 8 times. (40 sts)
Row 12: [Ssk, k3] 8 times. (32 sts)
Row 14: [Ssk, k2] 8 times. (24 sts)
Row 16: [Ssk, k1] 8 times. (16 sts)
Row 18: [Ssk] 8 times. (8 sts)
Row 19: Purl.
Break off yarn, leaving 20cm (8in) tail. Thread tail into a yarn needle and pass through remaining 8 sts. Tighten to close centre of disc.

FINISHING
Using tails of yarn, sew side edges of centre disc together to form a circle. Using sewing thread, sew beads evenly around centre disc just inside circle of yarn B and in line with each yarn C ridge (formed by the decreasing).

7 Cherry Twizzler
directory view page 35

Yarn: Aran-weight wool in red (A) and chartreuse (B) **Size:** Approx. 10cm (4in) diameter, using 4.5mm needles

METHOD
PETALS (make 11)
Using A, cast on 8 sts.
Cast off 7 sts to complete first petal. (1 st remains)
*Slip remaining st on to left needle and cast on 7 sts using knitted cast-on technique. (8 sts)
Cast off 7 sts. (1 st remains)*
Rep from * to * to make strip of 11 petals in total.
Break off yarn and pass through remaining stitch.
Either side of strip may be used as RS.

CENTRE DISC
Hold petal strip with unattached ends of petals hanging down. Using B and with RS facing, pick up and knit 2 sts from base of each petal along top edge of strip. (22 sts)
Row 1 (WS): [K3, ssk] 4 times, k2. (18 sts)
Row 2: Knit.
Row 3: [Ssk] 9 times. (9 sts)
Row 4: [Ssk] 4 times, k1. (5 sts)
Break off yarn, leaving 20cm (8in) tail. Thread tail into a yarn needle and pass through remaining 5 sts. Tighten to close centre of disc, then sew side edges of disc together to form a circle. Using A, join ends of petal strip.

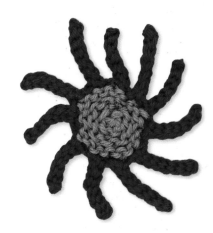

8 *Cocoa Sundrop*
directory view page 36

Yarn: Aran-weight wool in golden yellow (A) and maroon (B) **Size:** Approx. 16.5cm (6¹/₂in) diameter, using 4.5mm needles

METHOD
PETALS (make 8)
Using A, make eight small concave petals (see page 65).

CENTRE DISC
Using B and with RS facing, pick up and knit 3 sts from base of each petal. (24 sts)
Row 1 (WS): [K1, ssk] 8 times. (16 sts)
Row 2: Knit.
Row 3: [Ssk] 8 times. (8 sts)
Break off yarn, leaving 20cm (8in) tail. Thread tail into a yarn needle and pass through remaining 8 sts. Tighten to close centre of disc, then sew side edges of disc together to form a circle.

9 *Pompom Puff*
directory view page 40

Yarn: Aran-weight wool in variegated orange/rust (A), golden yellow (B) and orange (C)
Extras: 3.5cm (1³/₈in) diameter pompom maker; fabric glue (optional)
Size: Approx. 19cm (7¹/₂in) diameter, using 4.5mm needles

METHOD
CENTRE DISC
Using A, cast on 8 sts.
Row 1 (RS): Knit.
Rows 2, 4, 6 & 8: Knit.
Row 3: [Kfb] 8 times. (16 sts)
Row 5: [K1, kfb] 8 times. (24 sts)
Row 7: [K2, kfb] 8 times. (32 sts)
Row 9: [K3, kfb] 8 times. (40 sts)
Rows 10–12: Knit.
Row 13: [K3, k2tog] 8 times. (32 sts)
Rows 14, 16 & 18: Knit.
Row 15: [K2, k2tog] 8 times. (24 sts)
Row 17: [K1, k2tog] 8 times. (16 sts)
Row 19: [K2tog] 8 times. (8 sts)
Row 20: Knit.
Break off yarn, leaving 20cm (8in) tail. Thread tail into a yarn needle and pass through remaining 8 sts. Tighten to close centre of disc.

PETALS AND POMPOMS
Using B and leaving 20cm (8in) cast-on tails, make eleven small concave petals (see page 65). Using one strand each of B and C together, make six pompoms, leaving 20cm (8in) tails for easy tying (see page 23).

FINISHING
Using tail of yarn, sew side edges of centre disc together to form a hollow ball, leaving a small opening. Stuff with scraps of yarn A (or similar colour), then close the opening. Using cast-on tails, sew base of petals evenly spaced around back of centre disc. To attach a pompom, thread both tails separately through work at base of ring of petals. Tie the tails firmly with a flat knot and trim to about 6mm (¹/₄in). Arrange the pompoms evenly around centre disc. For extra security, paint the knots with fabric glue.

10 *Joker*
directory view page 38

Yarn: Aran-weight wool in orange (A), maroon (B) and variegated orange/rust (C)
Size: Approx. 19cm (7½in) diameter, using 4.5mm needles

METHOD
CENTRE DISC
Using A, cast on 8 sts.
Row 1 (RS): Knit.
Rows 2, 4, 6, 8 & 10: Knit.
Row 3: [Kfb] 8 times.
(16 sts)
Row 5: [K1, kfb] 8 times.
(24 sts)
Row 7: Purl.
Row 9: [K1, k2tog] 8 times.
(16 sts)
Row 11: [K2tog] 8 times.
(8 sts)
Row 12: Knit.
Break off yarn, leaving 20cm
(8in) tail. Thread tail into a
yarn needle and pass through
remaining 8 sts. Tighten to close
centre of disc.

LONG PETALS (make 9)
Using B and leaving 20cm (8in) cast-on tails,
make nine long veined petals, repeating rows
4–5 seven rather than five times (see page 65).

FRILLED PETALS (make 18)
Using C, cast on 5 sts.
Cast off 4 sts to complete first frilled petal.
(1 st remains)
*Slip remaining st on to left needle and cast on
4 sts using knitted cast-on technique. (5 sts)
Cast off 4 sts. (1 st remains)*
Rep from * to * to make strip of 18 frilled
petals in total.
Break off yarn, leaving 30cm (12in) tail, and pass
through remaining stitch.

FINISHING
Using tail of yarn, sew side edges of
centre disc together to form a hollow ball,
leaving a small opening. Stuff with scraps
of yarn A (or similar colour), then close
the opening. Using cast-on tails, sew base
of long petals evenly spaced around back
of centre disc. Using cast-off tail, sew
strip of frilled petals around disc, in front
of long petals.

11 *Toffee Twist*
directory view page 38

Yarn: DK-weight wool in burnt orange (A) and
purple (B) **Size:** Approx. 6cm (2¼in) diameter,
using 4mm needles

METHOD
PETALS (make 13)
Using A, cast on 5 sts.
Cast off 4 sts to complete first petal. (1 st remains)
*Slip remaining st on to left needle and cast on 4 sts
using knitted cast-on technique. (5 sts)
Cast off 4 sts. (1 st remains)*
Rep from * to * to make strip of 13 petals in total.
Break off yarn and pass through remaining stitch.
Either side of strip may be used as RS.

CENTRE DISC
Hold petal strip with unattached ends of petals hanging
down. Using B and with RS facing, pick up and knit
2 sts from base of each petal along top edge of strip.
(26 sts)
Row 1 (WS): [K2tog] 13 times. (13 sts)
Row 2: [K2tog] 6 times, k1. (7 sts)
Row 3: [K2tog] 3 times, k1. (4 sts)
Break off yarn, leaving 20cm (8in) tail. Thread tail
into a yarn needle and pass through remaining 4 sts.
Tighten to close centre of disc, then sew side edges
of disc together to form a circle. Using A, join ends
of petal strip.

12 *Woolly Mammoth*
directory view page 39

Yarn: Aran-weight wool in green (A), golden yellow (B), chartreuse (C) and orange (D)
Optional: Polyester toy stuffing
Size: Approx. 20cm (8in) diameter with petals spread open, using 4.5mm needles

METHOD
CENTRE DISC
Begin with stalk at back as follows:
Using A and leaving 20cm (8in) tail, cast on 9 sts.
Row 1 (RS): Knit.
Row 2 & all WS rows: Purl.
Row 3: Knit.
Row 5: [K3, m1] 3 times. (12 sts)
Row 7: [K4, m1] 3 times. (15 sts)
Row 9: [K5, m1] 3 times. (18 sts)
Row 11: [K6, m1] 3 times. (21 sts)
Row 13: [K7, m1] 3 times. (24 sts)
Row 15: [K4, m1] 6 times. (30 sts)
Row 17: [K5, m1] 6 times. (36 sts)
Row 19: [K6, m1] 6 times. (42 sts)
Row 21: [K7, m1] 6 times. (48 sts)
Row 23: [K6, m1] 8 times. (56 sts)
Row 25: [K7, m1] 8 times. (64 sts)
Row 26: Purl.
Break off A and join B.
Rows 27–28: Knit.
Row 29: Purl.
Repeat rows 28–29 three more times.
Rows 36–38: Knit.
Row 39: [K6, k2tog] 8 times. (56 sts)
Rows 40, 42 & 44: Knit.
Row 41: [K5, k2tog] 8 times. (48 sts)
Row 43: [K4, k2tog] 8 times. (40 sts)
Row 45: [K3, k2tog] 8 times. (32 sts)
Row 46: Knit.
Break off B and join C.
Row 47: [K2, k2tog] 8 times. (24 sts)
Rows 48 & 50: Purl.
Row 49: [K1, k2tog] 8 times. (16 sts)
Row 51: [K2tog] 8 times. (8 sts)
Row 52: Purl.
Break off yarn, leaving 20cm (8in) tail. Thread tail into a yarn needle and pass through remaining 8 sts. Tighten to close centre front of disc.

PETALS AND LEAVES
Leaving 20cm (8in) cast-on tails, make nine small veined petals using D (see page 65) and two thin veined leaves using A (see page 66).

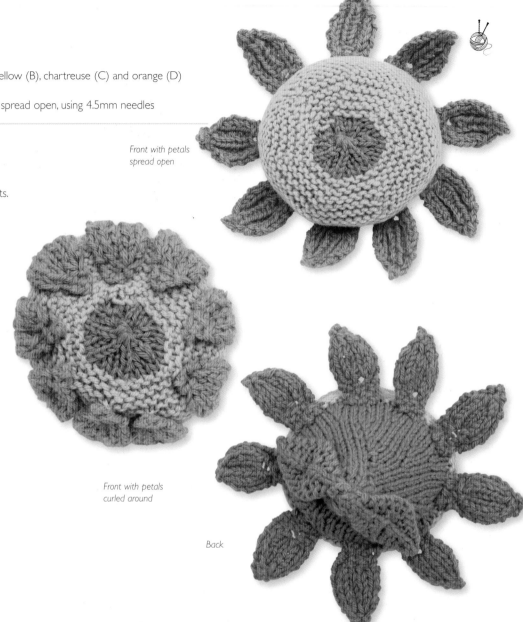

Front with petals spread open

Front with petals curled around

Back

FINISHING
Using tails of yarn, join seam of stalk at back of centre disc to form a hollow cone, leaving a small opening. Stuff with scraps of yarn (or use polyester toy stuffing since this is quite a large flower), then close the opening. Sew base of petals evenly spaced around centre disc, matching cast-on edges of petals to first row in yarn B on disc. The petals may be allowed to flop outwards, or stitched in place down centre so that they curl around disc. Sew a leaf on opposite sides of stem, attaching at base and with a few stitches halfway up centre of each leaf.

13 *Swizzle Sticks*
directory view page 48

Yarn: Aran-weight wool in pale gold (A), burnt orange (B), maroon (C) and pink (D)
Size: Approx. 14cm (5¹/₂in) diameter, using 4.5mm needles

METHOD
PETALS (make 3 layers)
Either side of layers may be used as RS.
Top layer: Using A, cast on 5 sts.
Cast off 4 sts to complete first petal.
(1 st remains)
*Slip remaining st on to left needle and
cast on 4 sts using knitted cast-on
technique. (5 sts)
Cast off 4 sts. (1 st remains)*
Rep from * to * to make strip of 13 petals
in total.
Break off yarn and pass through remaining stitch.
Middle layer: Using B, cast on 8 sts.
Cast off 7 sts to complete first petal.
(1 st remains)
*Slip remaining st on to left needle and cast on
7 sts using knitted cast-on technique. (8 sts)
Cast off 7 sts. (1 st remains)*
Rep from * to * to make strip of 13 petals
in total.
Break off yarn and pass through remaining stitch.
Bottom layer: Using C, cast on 11 sts.
Cast off 10 sts to complete first petal.
(1 st remains)
*Slip remaining st on to left needle and cast on
10 sts using knitted cast-on technique. (11 sts)
Cast off 10 sts. (1 st remains)*

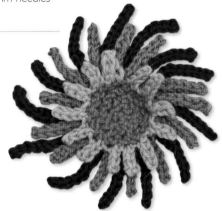

Rep from * to * to make strip of 13
petals in total.
Break off yarn and pass through
remaining stitch.

CENTRE DISC
Hold top layer petal strip with unattached
ends of petals hanging down. Using D and
with RS facing, pick up and knit 2 sts from
base of each petal along top edge of strip.
(26 sts)
Row 1 (WS): [K11, ssk] twice. (24 sts)
Row 2: [Ssk, k1] 8 times. (16 sts)
Row 3: Knit.
Row 4: [Ssk] 8 times. (8 sts)
Row 5: Knit.
Break off yarn, leaving 20cm (8in) tail.
Thread tail into a yarn needle and pass
through remaining 8 sts. Tighten to close
centre of disc, then sew side edges of disc
together to form a circle.

FINISHING
Pin middle petal layer behind top petal
layer and sew to back around outer edge
of centre disc. Attach bottom petal layer
in same way.

*Felted variation with
bottom petal layer omitted.*

14 *Prairie Gold*
directory view page 45

Yarn: DK-weight wool in golden yellow (A) and
orange (B) **Size:** Approx. 9cm (3¹/₂in) diameter,
using 4mm needles

METHOD
PETALS (make 17)
Using A, cast on 10 sts.
Cast off 9 sts to complete first petal. (1 st remains)
*Slip remaining st on to left needle and cast on 9 sts
using knitted cast-on technique. (10 sts)
Cast off 9 sts. (1 st remains)*
Rep from * to * to make strip of 17 petals in total.
Break off yarn and pass through remaining stitch.
Either side of strip may be used as RS.

CENTRE DISC
Hold petal strip with unattached ends of petals hanging
down. Using B and with RS facing, pick up and knit
2 sts from base of each petal along top edge of strip.
(34 sts)
Row 1 (WS): Knit.
Row 2: [K1, k2tog] 11 times, k1. (23 sts)
Row 3: Knit.
Row 4: [K2tog] 11 times, k1. (12 sts)
Row 5: [K2tog] 6 times. (6 sts)
Row 6: [K2tog] 3 times. (3 sts)
Break off yarn, leaving 20cm (8in) tail. Thread tail
into a yarn needle and pass through remaining 3 sts.
Tighten to close centre of disc, then sew side edges
of disc together to form a circle. Using A, join ends
of petal strip.

15 Gold Stripe
directory view page 49

Yarn: Aran-weight wool in brown tweed (A), golden yellow (B) and burnt orange (C)
Size: Approx. 20cm (8in) diameter, using 4.5mm needles

METHOD
CENTRE DISC
Using A, cast on 42 sts.
Row 1 (WS): Knit.
Row 2: K1, [k3, k2tog] 8 times, k1. (34 sts)
Row 3: K1, [(k1, p1, k1) in next st, p3tog] 8 times, k1.
Row 4: Purl. Without breaking off A, join B.
Row 5: Using B, k1, [p3tog, (k1, p1, k1) in next st] 8 times, k1.
Row 6: Using B, purl. Break off B and continue in A.
Rows 7–8: As rows 3–4 (so ending with a RS row). Break off yarn and slip all sts on to other needle, so next row will also be a RS row. Join C.
Row 9 (RS): Ssk, k to last 2 sts, k2tog. (32 sts)
Row 10: Knit.
Row 11: [Ssk] 16 times. (16 sts)
Row 12: Knit.
Row 13: [Ssk] 8 times. (8 sts)
Row 14: Knit.
Break off yarn, leaving 20cm (8in) tail. Thread tail into a yarn needle and pass through remaining 8 sts. Tighten to close centre of disc.

PETALS (make 8)
Using C and leaving 20cm (8in) cast-on tails, make eight large garter petals (see page 64).

FINISHING
Using tails of yarn, sew side edges of disc together to form a circle. Steam disc to make it lie flat, without losing texture of stitches. Sew base of petals around back of row 4 of centre disc, spacing them evenly at angles created by the decreasing.

16 Sweet Petite
directory view page 42

Yarn: Aran-weight wool in pink (A) and maroon (B) **Size:** Approx. 7.5cm (3in) diameter, using 4.5mm needles

METHOD
PETALS (make 9)
Using A, cast on 5 sts.
Cast off 4 sts to complete first petal. (1 st remains)
*Slip remaining st on to left needle and cast on 4 sts using knitted cast-on technique. (5 sts)
Cast off 4 sts. (1 st remains)*
Rep from * to * to make strip of 9 petals in total.
Break off yarn and pass through remaining stitch.
Either side of strip may be used as RS.

CENTRE DISC
Hold petal strip with unattached ends of petals hanging down. Using B and with RS facing, pick up and knit 2 sts from base of each petal along top edge of strip. (18 sts)
Row 1 (WS): Knit.
Row 2: [Ssk] 9 times. (9 sts)
Row 3: [Ssk] 4 times, k1. (5 sts)
Break off yarn, leaving 20cm (8in) tail. Thread tail into a yarn needle and pass through remaining 5 sts. Tighten to close centre of disc, then sew side edges of disc together to form a circle. Using A, join ends of petal strip.

17 *Lazy Daisy*
directory view page 46

Yarn: Aran-weight wool in green (A), taupe (B), pale gold (C) and orange (D)
Size: Approx. 22cm (8³/₄in) diameter, using 4.5mm needles

METHOD

CENTRE DISC

Begin at centre back as follows:
Using A, cast on 8 sts.
Row 1 (WS): Knit.
Row 2: [Kfb] 8 times. (16 sts)
Row 3: Knit.
Row 4: [K1, kfb] 8 times. (24 sts)
Row 5: Knit.
Row 6: [K2, kfb] 8 times. (32 sts)
Row 7: Knit.
Break off A and join B.
Rows 8–9: Knit.
Without breaking off B, join C.
Row 10: Using C, [k3tog, (k1, p1, k1) in next st] 8 times.
Row 11: Using C, knit.
Break off C and continue in B.
Row 12: [(K1, p1, k1) in next st, k3tog] 8 times.
Row 13: Knit.
Break off B and join D.
Rows 14–15: Knit.
Row 16: [K2, k2tog] 8 times. (24 sts)
Row 17: Knit.
Row 18: [K1, k2tog] 8 times. (16 sts)
Row 19: Knit.
Row 20: [K2tog] 8 times. (8 sts)
Row 21: Knit.
Break off yarn, leaving 20cm (8in) tail. Thread tail into a yarn needle and pass through remaining 8 sts. Tighten to close centre of disc.

PETALS (make 9)

Using C, make nine medium concave petals (see page 65). Using C and with RS facing, pick up and knit 7 sts from base of each petal. (63 sts)
Row 1 (WS): Knit.
Row 2: [K2tog] 31 times, k1. (32 sts)
Cast off, leaving 25cm (10in) tail, and use this tail to sew row ends together to form a circle of petals.

FINISHING

Using tails of yarn, sew side edges of centre disc together to form a hollow ball, leaving a small opening. Stuff with scraps of matching yarn, then close the opening. Sew circle of petals evenly spaced around back of centre disc, joining to last row of disc worked in yarn A. Using double strand of D, work a 2.5cm (1in) long lazy daisy stitch at base of each petal (see page 26).

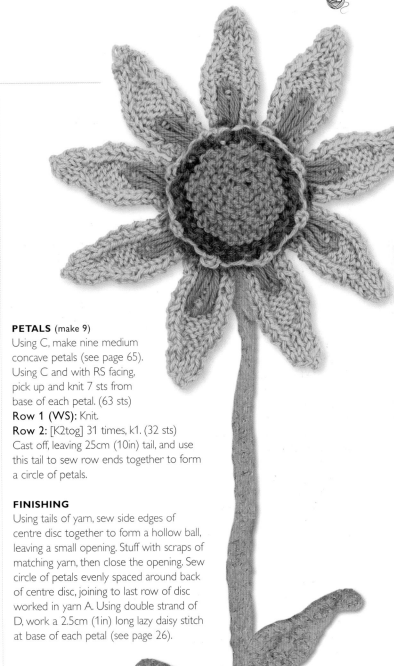

18 Bobble Beauty
directory view page 42

Yarn: Aran-weight cotton in burgundy (A), green (B) and pink (C)
Size: Approx. 15cm (6in) diameter, using 4.5mm needles

METHOD
Note: MB5 = make 5-st bobble
(see page 15).

CENTRE DISC
Using A, cast on 28 sts.
Row 1 (WS): K1, [MB5, k3]
6 times, MB5, k2.
Rows 2–3: Knit.
Break off A and join B.
Rows 4–5: Knit.
Row 6: [K5, k2tog] 4 times.
(24 sts)
Row 7: Knit.
Row 8: [K1, k2tog] 8 times. (16 sts)
Row 9: Knit.
Row 10: [K2tog] 8 times. (8 sts)
Row 11: Knit.
Break off yarn, leaving 20cm (8in) tail. Thread tail into a yarn needle and
pass through remaining 8 sts. Tighten to close centre of disc.

PETALS (make 7)
Using C and leaving 20cm (8in) cast-on tails, make seven medium garter
petals (see page 64).

FINISHING
Using tails of yarn, join side edges of
centre disc together to form a circle.
If necessary, use tip of yarn needle
to pull bobbles to RS of disc.
Sew base of petals evenly
spaced around back of
centre disc.

*Felted variation
worked in wool yarn.*

19 Pompom Gem
directory view page 37

Yarn: Aran-weight wool in red (A), golden yellow (B) and orange (C)
Extras: 3.5cm (1³/₈in) diameter pompom maker; fabric glue (optional)
Size: Approx. 12.5cm (5in) diameter, using 4.5mm needles

METHOD
PETALS (make 6)
Using A, make six medium garter petals (see page 64).

CENTRE DISC
Using A and with RS facing, pick up and knit 5 sts from base of each
petal. (30 sts)
Row 1 (WS): [K2tog] 15 times. (15 sts)
Row 2: Knit.
Row 3: [K2tog] 7 times, k1. (8 sts)
Break off yarn, leaving 20cm (8in) tail. Thread tail into a yarn needle and
pass through remaining 8 sts. Tighten to close centre of disc, then sew
side edges of disc together to form a circle.

POMPOM
Using one strand each of B and C together, make a pompom, leaving
20cm (8in) tails for easy tying (see page 23). Thread both tails separately
through centre disc, tie firmly with a flat knot and trim to about 6mm
(¹/₄in). For extra security, paint the knots with fabric glue.

*Felted variation with petals
and centre disc worked
in different colours, and
French knot embroidery
instead of a pompom.*

20 *Amethyst Queen*
directory view page 44

Yarn: Aran-weight wool in burnt orange (A), dark grey (B), pink (C) and purple (D)
Size: Approx. 28cm (11in) diameter, using 4.5mm needles

METHOD
Note: MB5 = make 5-st bobble (see page 15).

CENTRE DISC
Using A, cast on 40 sts.
Row 1 (WS): [K3, k2tog] 8 times. (32 sts)
Rows 2–3: Knit.
Break off A and join B.
Row 4: [K2, k2tog] 8 times. (24 sts)
Row 5: K1, [MB5, k3] 5 times, MB5, k2.
Row 6: Knit.
Row 7: [K3, MB5] 6 times.
Break off B and join C.
Rows 8–9: Knit.
Row 10: [K1, k2tog] 8 times. (16 sts)
Row 11: Knit.
Row 12: [K2tog] 8 times. (8 sts)
Row 13: Knit.
Break off yarn, leaving 20cm (8in) tail.
Thread tail into a yarn needle and pass through remaining 8 sts.
Tighten to close centre of disc.

PETALS (make 11)
Using D, make eleven large concave petals (see page 65).

Using D and with RS facing, pick up and knit 7 sts from base of each petal. (77 sts)
Row 1 (WS): Knit.
To cast off: [K2tog] twice (2 sts on right needle), lift first st made over second st and off right needle, *k2tog (2 sts on right needle), lift previous st over new st and off right needle.* Repeat from * to * to end.
Break off D, leaving 25cm (10in) tail, and pass through remaining stitch. Use tail to sew row ends together to form a circle.

FINISHING
Use tails of yarn, sew side edges of centre disc together to form a circle. Sew circle of petals to back of disc.

21 *Catherine Wheel*
directory view page 45

Yarn: Aran-weight cotton in lemon yellow (A), red (B) and purple (C) **Size:** Approx. 11.5cm (4¹/₂in) diameter, using 4.5mm needles

METHOD
Note: MB3 = make 3-st bobble (see page 15).

CENTRE DISC AND PETALS
Using A, cast on 48 sts.
Row 1 (WS): [MB3, k7] 6 times.
Row 2: [K6, k2tog] 6 times. (42 sts)
Row 3: [MB3, p6] 6 times.
Row 4: [K5, k2tog] 6 times. (36 sts)
Row 5: [MB3, p5] 6 times.
Row 6: [K4, k2tog] 6 times. (30 sts)
Row 7: [MB3, p4] 6 times.
Row 8: [K3, k2tog] 6 times. (24 sts)
Row 9: [MB3, p3] 6 times.
Row 10: [K2, k2tog] 6 times. (18 sts)
Break off A and join B.
Row 11: Purl.
Row 12: [P1, p2tog] 6 times. (12 sts)
Row 13: Purl.
Row 14: [P2tog] 6 times. (6 sts)
Row 15: Purl.
Break off yarn, leaving 20cm (8in) tail.
Thread tail into a yarn needle and pass through remaining 6 sts. Tighten to close centre of disc.

FINISHING
Using tails of yarn, sew side edges together to form a circle. Using double strand of C, work French knots around centre disc (see page 26).

22 *Flower Back and Stem*

directory view pages 34, 45, 47 & 49

Yarn: Aran-weight wool in green **Extras:** Two double-pointed needles (dpn) to work i-cord stem (use two sizes smaller than recommended size for yarn) **Size:** Cone approx. 9cm (3½in) diameter, using 4.5mm needles; stem length as required

METHOD

Note: For a smaller cone to fit back of smaller flower, cast off after row 11, 15 or 19, or use finer yarn and correspondingly smaller needles. For a larger cone, see instructions below or use heavier yarn and correspondingly larger needles.

STEM

Using dpn, cast on 4, 5 or 6 sts, depending on how thick you want the stem to be. Work an i-cord to length required (see page 15), then cast off.
To make a stem using ordinary single-pointed needles, cast on enough sts for length of stem required. For a flat stem, knit two rows and then cast off.
For a round stem, knit number of rows required for desired width of stem, then cast off; fold stem in half lengthways and sew long edges together.

CONE

Using single-pointed needles, cast on 6 sts.
Rows 1–3: Knit.
Row 4: [Kfb] 6 times. (12 sts)
Row 5: Knit.
Row 6: K1, [m1, k2] 5 times, m1, k1. (18 sts)
Rows 7–9: Knit.
Row 10: K1, [m1, k3] 5 times, m1, k2. (24 sts)
Rows 11–13: Knit.
Row 14: K1, [m1, k4] 5 times, m1, k3. (30 sts)
Rows 15–17: Knit.
Row 18: K1, [m1, k5] 5 times, m1, k4. (36 sts)
Rows 19–21: Knit.
Row 22: K1, [m1, k6] 5 times, m1, k5. (42 sts)
Rows 23–24: Knit.
For a larger cone to fit back of larger flower, continue in this way, working an increase row on 2nd and every following 4th row.
Cast off, leaving tail of yarn for sewing to flower.

FINISHING

Sew seam of cone, then sew top of stem to back of cone. Stuff cone with scraps of matching yarn and sew to back of sunflower.

Flower back with i-cord stem.

23 *Garter Petals*

directory view page 49

Yarn: Aran-weight wool in petal colour
Sizes: Approx. length: small 4cm (1½in); medium 5cm (2in); large 6cm (2½in); all using 4.5mm needles

METHOD

Note: Either side of petals may be used as RS.

SMALL

Cast on 3 sts.
Rows 1–2: Knit.
Row 3: Kfb, k1, kfb. (5 sts)
Rows 4–6: Knit.
Row 7: K1, cdd, k1. (3 sts)
Rows 8–10: Knit.
Row 11: Cdd. (1 st)
Break off yarn and pass through remaining stitch.

Small

MEDIUM

Cast on 5 sts.
Row 1: Knit.
Row 2 and all even rows: Knit.
Row 3: Kfb, k3, kfb. (7 sts)
Row 5: Kfb, k5, kfb. (9 sts)
Row 7: Knit.
Row 9: K3, cdd, k3. (7 sts)
Row 11: K2, cdd, k2. (5 sts)
Row 13: K1, cdd, k1. (3 sts)
Row 15: Cdd. (1 st)
Break off yarn and pass through remaining stitch.

Medium

LARGE

Cast on 3 sts.
Rows 1–2: Knit.
Row 3: Kfb, k1, kfb. (5 sts)
Row 4: Kfb, k3, kfb. (7 sts)
Rows 5–12: Knit.
Row 13: K2, cdd, k2. (5 sts)
Row 14: Knit.
Row 15: K1, cdd, k1. (3 sts)
Row 16: Knit.
Row 17: Cdd. (1 st)
Break off yarn and pass through remaining stitch.

Large

24 Concave Petals
directory view page 49

Yarn: Aran-weight wool in petal colour
Sizes: Approx. length: small 6.5cm (2½in); medium 8cm (3¼in); large 10cm (4in); all using 4.5mm needles

METHOD
Note: Do not block the petals because this will flatten the concave shape.

SMALL
Cast on 3 sts.
Row 1 (RS): Knit.
Row 2: Knit.
Row 3: Kfb, p1, kfb. (5 sts)
Row 4: P2, k1, p2.
Row 5: K2, (k1, yo, k1, yo, k1) in next st, k2. (9 sts)
Rows 6, 8 & 10: P2, k5, p2.
Rows 7 & 9: K2, p5, k2.
Row 11: Ssk, k1, p3, k1, k2tog. (7 sts)
Row 12: P2, k3, p2.
Row 13: K2, p3tog, k2. (5 sts)
Rows 14 & 16: Purl.
Row 15: Ssk, k1, k2tog. (3 sts)
Row 17: Cdd. (1 st)
Break off yarn and pass through remaining stitch.

MEDIUM
Cast on 7 sts.
Row 1 (RS): K2, p3, k2.
Row 2: P2, k3, p2.
Rows 3–4: As rows 1–2.
Row 5: K2, m1, p3, m1, k2. (9 sts)
Rows 6, 8 & 10: P2, k5, p2.
Rows 7 & 9: K2, p5, k2.
Row 11: K1, ssk, p3, k2tog, k1. (7 sts)
Row 12: P2, k3, p2.
Row 13: K1, ssk, p1, k2tog, k1. (5 sts)
Rows 14 & 16: Purl.
Row 15: Knit.

Row 17: Ssk, k1, k2tog. (3 sts)
Row 18: P3tog. (1 st)
Break off yarn and pass through remaining stitch.

LARGE
Cast on 7 sts.
Rows 1–5: As for medium petal.
Rows 6, 8, 10 & 12: P2, k5, p2.
Rows 7, 9 & 11: K2, p5, k2.
Row 13: K1, ssk, p3, k2tog, k1. (7 sts)
Row 14: P2, k3, p2.
Row 15: K2, p3, k2.
Rows 16–17: As rows 14–15.
Row 18: As row 14.
Row 19: K2, p3tog, k2. (5 sts)
Row 20: P2, k1, p2.
Row 21: K2, p1, k2.
Rows 22 & 24: Purl.
Row 23: K1, cdd, k1. (3 sts)
Row 25: Cdd. (1 st)
Break off yarn and pass through remaining stitch.

Small

Medium

Large

25 Veined Petals
directory view page 40

Yarn: Aran-weight wool in petal colour
Sizes: Approx. length: small 6cm (2¼in); long 8cm (3¼in); both using 4.5mm needles

METHOD
SMALL
Cast on 3 sts.
Rows 1–5: As for small concave petal (see left).
Row 6 (RS): P2, k2, p1, k2, p2.
Row 7: K2, p2, k1, p2, k2.
Rows 8–9: As rows 6–7.
Row 10: As row 6.
Row 11: Ssk, p2, k1, p2, k2tog. (7 sts)
Row 12: P1, ssk, p1, k2tog, p1. (5 sts)
Row 13: K1, cdd, k1. (3 sts)
Row 14: Purl.
Row 15: Cdd. (1 st)
Break off yarn and pass through remaining stitch.

LONG
Cast on 3 sts.
Row 1 (RS): Knit.
Row 2: Kfb, p1, kfb. (5 sts)
Row 3: Knit.
Row 4: K2, p1, k2.
Row 5: Knit.
Repeat rows 4–5 five more times. (15 rows in total; length of petal may be varied here)
Row 16: Ssk, k1, k2tog. (3 sts)
Row 17: K1, p1, k1.
Row 18: Cdd. (1 st)
Break off yarn and pass through remaining stitch.

Small

Long

Veined Leaves

26

directory view pages 34, 38 & 43

Yarn: Aran-weight wool in green

Sizes: Approx. length: small 4.5cm (1³/₄in); medium 7cm (2³/₄in); large 10cm (4in); thin 8.5cm (3¹/₄in); all using 4.5mm needles

METHOD

SMALL

Cast on 1 st.

Row 1 (RS): Knit into front, purl into back and knit into front of st. (3 sts)

Row 2: K1, p1, k1.

Row 3: Kfb, k1, kfb. (5 sts)

Row 4: K2, p1, k2.

Row 5: Knit.

Rows 6–7: As rows 4–5.

Row 8: As row 4.

Row 9: K1, cdd, k1. (3 sts)

Row 10: K1, p1, k1.

Row 11: Cdd. (1 st)

Break off yarn and pass through remaining stitch.

Medium

MEDIUM

Cast on 1 st.

Row 1 (WS): Knit.

Row 2: Knit into front, purl into back and knit into front of st. (3 sts)

Row 3: K1, p1, k1.

Row 4: Kfb, k1, kfb. (5 sts)

Row 5: K2, p1, k2.

Row 6: Kfb, k3, kfb. (7 sts)

Row 7: K3, p1, k3.

Row 8: Kfb, k5, kfb. (9 sts)

Row 9: K4, p1, k4.

Row 10: Knit.

Repeat rows 9–10 twice more.

Row 15: As row 9.

Small

Row 16: K3, cdd, k3. (7 sts)

Row 17: K3, p1, k3.

Row 18: K2, cdd, k2. (5 sts)

Row 19: K2, p1, k2.

Row 20: K1, cdd, k1. (3 sts)

Row 21: K1, p1, k1.

Row 22: Cdd. (1 st)

Break off yarn and pass through remaining stitch.

Large

LARGE

Cast on 1 st.

Row 1 (WS): Knit.

Row 2: Knit into front, purl into back and knit into front of st. (3 sts)

Row 3: K1, p1, k1.

Row 4: Kfb, k1, kfb. (5 sts)

Row 5: K2, p1, k2.

Row 6: Kfb, k3, kfb. (7 sts)

Row 7: K3, p1, k3.

Row 8: Kfb, k5, kfb. (9 sts)

Row 9: K4, p1, k4.

Row 10: Kfb, k7, kfb. (11 sts)

Row 11: K5, p1, k5.

Row 12: Kfb, k9, kfb. (13 sts)

Row 13: K6, p1, k6.

Row 14: Knit.

Repeat rows 13–14 three more times.

Row 21: As row 13.

Row 22: K5, cdd, k5. (11 sts)

Row 23: K5, p1, k5.

Row 24: K4, cdd, k4. (9 sts)

Row 25: K4, p1, k4.

Row 26: K3, cdd, k3. (7 sts)

Row 27: K3, p1, k3.

Row 28: K2, cdd, k2. (5 sts)

Row 29: K2, p1, k2.

Row 30: K1, cdd, k1. (3 sts)

Row 31: K1, p1, k1.

Row 32: Cdd. (1 st)

Break off yarn and pass through remaining stitch.

Thin

THIN

Cast on 1 st.

Row 1 (RS): Knit into front, back and front of st. (3 sts)

Row 2: K1, p1, k1.

Row 3: Knit.

Row 4: K1, p1, k1.

Row 5: K1, m1, k1, m1, k1. (5 sts)

Row 6: K2, p1, k2.

Row 7: Knit.

Row 8: K2, p1, k2.

Row 9: K2, m1, k1, m1, k2. (7 sts)

Rows 10, 12, 14 & 16: K3, p1, k3.

Rows 11, 13 & 15: Knit.

Row 17: K2, cdd, k2. (5 sts)

Row 18: K2, p1, k2.

Row 19: Knit.

Row 20: K2, p1, k2.

Row 21: K1, cdd, k1. (3 sts)

Row 22: K1, p1, k1.

Row 23: Cdd. (1 st)

Break off yarn and pass through remaining stitch.

27 *Jagged Leaves*
directory view pages 35, 41 & 45

Yarn: Aran-weight wool in green
Size: Approx. 11cm (4¼in) long, using 4.5mm needles

METHOD
PICOT EDGING
Make a large veined leaf (see page 66).
Work right and left edges separately, with four picots along each edge, as follows:

Right edge: With RS facing, pick up and knit 1 st from centre st at bottom point of leaf, 16 sts along right edge up to top of leaf and 1 st from cast-off st at top point. (18 sts)

Picot cast-off (WS): Cast off 2 sts, *slip 1 st from right needle on to left needle, cast 2 sts on to left needle using knitted cast-on technique, cast off 5 sts (the two just added, then the next three); rep from * three more times, then cast off rem sts.

Left edge: With RS facing, pick up and knit 1 st from side of right-edge picot cast-off row, 1 st from top point of leaf, 16 sts along left edge down to bottom of leaf, 1 st from centre st at bottom point and 1 st from side of right-edge picot cast-off row. (20 sts)

Picot cast-off (WS): Cast off 5 sts, *slip 1 st from right needle on to left needle, cast 2 sts on to left needle using knitted cast-on technique, cast off 5 sts (the two just added, then the next three); rep from * three more times, then cast off rem sts.

Mix and match textures and shapes, such as jagged-edged leaves teamed with the pointed petals and fluffy centre of Pompom Gem (page 62).

BOBBLE EDGING
Make a large veined leaf (see page 66).
Work right and left edges separately, with four bobbles along each edge, as follows:

Right edge: With RS facing, pick up and knit 18 sts as for picot edging.

Bobble cast-off (WS): *Cast off 2 sts, (k1, p1, k1) in next st, turn, p3, turn, k3, lift second and third sts on right needle over first st to complete bobble, then cast off this st; rep from * three more times, then cast off rem sts.

Left edge: With RS facing, pick up and knit 20 sts as for picot edging.

Bobble cast-off (WS): Cast off 3 sts, *cast off 2 sts, (k1, p1, k1) in next st, turn, p3, turn, k3, lift second and third sts on right needle over first st to complete bobble, then cast off this st; rep from * three more times, then cast off rem sts.

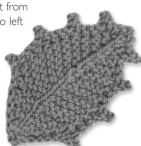

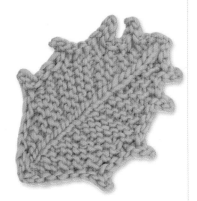

Two picot-edged leaves worked in different weights of yarn. The top one is worked in Aran-weight yarn, while the bottom one is worked in chunky-weight yarn using 5.5mm needles to make a leaf approx. 15cm (6in) long.

Two bobble-edged leaves worked in different colours but same weight of yarn.

Swallowtail Butterfly

directory view page 44

Yarn: Aran-weight cotton in lemon yellow (A); aran-weight wool in black (B) and blue (C)
Extras: Two 6mm (¼in) round black beads for eyes; black sewing thread and needle; fabric glue (optional)
Size: Approx. 14cm (5½in) wingspan, using 4.5mm needles

METHOD

LEFT WING

Using A, cast on 9 sts.
Row 1 (WS): Knit.
Row 2: Kfb, k7, kfb. (11 sts)
Rows 3, 5, 7, 9 & 11: Knit.
Row 4: K2tog, place marker (decreases for wing shaping will be worked on marker side), k9. (10 sts)
Row 6: K2tog, k8. (9 sts)
Row 8: K2tog, k7. (8 sts)
Row 10: K2tog, k6. (7 sts)
Row 12: K2tog, k3, turn leaving 2 sts unworked.
Row 13: Slip 1, k3 to end.
Row 14: K2tog, k4. (5 sts)
Rows 15, 17 & 19: Knit.
Row 16: K2tog, k3. (4 sts)
Row 18: K2tog, k2. (3 sts)
Row 20: K2tog, k1. (2 sts)
Row 21: Knit.
Cast off.

The swallowtails at the base of each wing are worked as part of the wing edging.

RIGHT WING

Using A, cast on 9 sts.
Row 1 (WS): Knit.
Row 2: Kfb, k7, kfb. (11 sts)
Rows 3, 5, 7, 9 & 11: Knit.
Row 4: K9, place marker (decreases for wing shaping will be worked on marker side), k2tog. (10 sts)
Row 6: K8, ssk. (9 sts)
Row 8: K7, ssk. (8 sts)
Row 10: K6, ssk. (7 sts)
Row 12: K5, ssk. (6 sts)
Row 13: K4, turn leaving 2 sts unworked.
Row 14: Slip 1, k1, ssk.
Row 15: Knit. (5 sts)
Row 16: K3, ssk. (4 sts)
Row 17: Knit.
Row 18: K2, ssk. (3 sts)
Row 19: Knit.
Row 20: K1, ssk. (2 sts)
Row 21: Knit.
Cast off.

RIGHT-WING EDGING

Using B and with RS facing, pick up and knit 11 sts along top (cast-on) edge of wing. Cast off knitwise.
Using B and with RS facing, pick up and knit 2 sts from cast-off sts at bottom of wing, 11 sts up right edge and 1 st from side of top edging. (14 sts)
Row 1 (WS): K14.
Row 2: K3, turn.
Row 3: Slip 1, k2.
Row 4: To make swallowtail, cast 4 sts on to left needle using knitted cast-on technique, cast off 4 sts (1 st on right needle); k13 to end.
Cast off knitwise.

LEFT-WING EDGING

Using B and with RS facing, pick up and knit 11 sts along top (cast-on) edge of wing. Cast off knitwise.

Using B and with RS facing, pick up and knit 1 st from left side of top edging, 11 sts down left edge and 2 sts from cast-off sts at bottom of wing. (14 sts)

Row 1 (WS): K3, turn.

Row 2: Slip 1, k2.

Row 3: K14 to end.

Row 4: K14; to make swallowtail, cast 4 sts on to left needle using knitted cast-on technique, cast off 4 sts (1 st on right needle). Cast off knitwise to end.

BODY

Using B, cast on 3 sts.

Row 1 (RS): Knit.

Row 2 & all WS rows: Purl.

Row 3: Kfb, k1, kfb. (5 sts)

Row 5: Kfb, k3, kfb. (7 sts)

Row 7: Knit.

Row 9: Kfb, k5, kfb. (9 sts)

Row 11: Knit.

Continue in stocking stitch (knit RS, purl WS) until body measures same length as inner (unfinished) edges of wings (including swallowtails).

Shape head as follows:

Next row: K2tog, k5, ssk. (7 sts)

Next row: Purl.

Next row: K2tog, k3, ssk. (5 sts)

Next row: P2tog, p1, p2tog. (3 sts)

Next row: Knit.

Break off yarn and pass through remaining 3 sts.

FINISHING

Using B, fold body in half lengthways and sew seam, stuffing body lightly with scraps of yarn as you do so. Sew wings on either side of body. Using double strand of A, work running stitch along sides of wings, through the edging (see page 26). Work two long straight stitches at either side of head. Using double strand of B, work long straight stitches at upper edge of each wing, decreasing in length towards outer edge of wings. Using double strand of C, work random straight stitches at lower edge of each wing. Using sewing thread, sew a bead at each side of head for eyes. Using single strand of B, add antennae at top of head, above the eyes (see page 23). Trim antennae to about 2.5cm (1in) and stiffen with fabric glue if desired.

Use the photographs as a guide for working the embroidery stitches.

29 *Honey Bee*
directory view page 42

Yarn: Aran-weight wool in brown tweed (A) and amber (B) **Extras:** 0.3mm (28-gauge) galvanised steel wire or jewellery wire for wings; two 8mm (³/₈in) round brown wooden beads for eyes; brown sewing thread and needle; four black hair grips for legs and antennae; wire clippers; round-nose pliers; glue suitable for use with metal **Size:** Approx. 10cm (4in) long, using 4.5mm needles

METHOD
BODY
Using A, cast on 3 sts.
Row 1 (RS): Knit.
Row 2: Purl.
Row 3: [Kfb] 3 times. (6 sts)
Row 4: Purl.
Row 5: Kfb, k4, kfb. (8 sts)
Row 6: Purl.
Without breaking off A, join B.
Row 7: Using B, kfb, k6, kfb. (10 sts)
Row 8: Using B, purl.
Row 9: Using A, kfb, k8, kfb. (12 sts)
Row 10: Using A, purl.
Row 11: Using B, knit.
Row 12: Using B, purl.
Row 13: Using A, knit.
Row 14: Using A, [p2tog] 6 times. (6 sts)
Row 15: Using A, knit.
Row 16: Using A, purl.
Break off A and continue in B.
Row 17: [Kfb] 6 times. (12 sts)
Row 18: Purl.

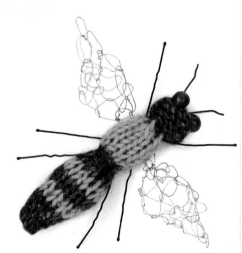

Work running stitch around the waist (row 15) and neck (row 24) to pull the bee's body into shape.

Row 19: Knit.
Row 20: Purl.
Rows 21–22: As rows 19–20.
Row 23: [K2tog] 6 times. (6 sts)
Break off B and rejoin A.
Row 24: Purl.
Row 25: [Kfb] 6 times. (12 sts)
Row 26 (WS): Knit.
Row 27: Purl.
Row 28: Knit.
Row 29: Purl.
Row 30: [K2tog] 6 times. (6 sts)
Break off yarn, leaving 20cm (8in) tail. Thread tail into a yarn needle and pass through remaining 6 sts. Tighten to close top of head.

WINGS (make 2)
Using wire, cast on 2 sts.
Rows 1–2: Knit.
Row 3: K1, lift strand lying before next st and knit into it, k1. (3 sts)
Row 4: Knit.
Row 5: K1, k2tog. (2 sts)
Row 6: K2tog. (1 st)
Cut wire, leaving 25cm (10in) tail. Pass through remaining stitch and weave along side edge to cast-on edge. Bend to resemble a bee wing.

Pull the wire wings into the desired shape, and make sure that any sharp ends are neatened and tucked into the bee's body.

FINISHING
Fold body in half lengthways and sew seam, stuffing body with scraps of yarn A (or similar colour) as you do so. Using A, work running stitch around waist and neck decreases (see page 26), then gather tightly and secure. Using sewing thread, sew on beads for eyes at top of head. Use pliers to bend hair grips into the shape of three pairs of legs and a pair of antennae, trimming with wire clippers. Thread legs through bee's body and antennae through head between eyes. To steady them, apply a small amount of glue to the points that join the knitted piece. Attach a wing at each side of body by threading the tails of wire securely through body. To neaten ends of wire and avoid sharp points, cut away the excess wire, then wind the tip back on itself for about 3mm (¹/₈in) and squeeze with pliers. Push the wire ends into the body.

30 *Woolly Bear Caterpillar*
directory view page 39

Yarn: For small caterpillar: fringed yarn in black (A) and copper (B); for large caterpillar: fringed yarn in black used double (A), and in copper and orange used together (B); smooth black yarn for sewing seams **Optional:** 1mm (18-gauge) galvanised steel wire or jewellery wire; wire clippers; round-nose pliers
Sizes: Small caterpillar approx. 8cm (3¼in) long, using 3.75mm needles; large caterpillar 14cm (5½in) long, using 5.5mm needles

METHOD
Note: The small caterpillar is worked using a single strand of yarn throughout, in the usual way. The large caterpillar is worked using two strands of yarn together throughout – two strands of black for A, and one strand each of copper and orange for B – and correspondingly larger needles.

BOTH CATERPILLARS
Using A, cast on 5 sts.
Row 1 (RS): Knit.
Row 2: Purl.
Row 3: [Kfb] 5 times. (10 sts)
Row 4: Purl.
Row 5: Knit.
Row 6: Purl.
Break off A and join B.
Rows 7, 9, 11, 13 & 15: Knit.
Rows 8, 10, 12, 14 & 16: Purl.
Break off B and rejoin A.
Rows 17, 19, 21 & 23: Knit.
Rows 18, 20, 22 & 24: Purl.
Row 25: [K2tog] 5 times. (5 sts)
Break off yarn, leaving 15cm (6in) tail. Thread tail into a yarn needle and pass through remaining 5 sts. Tighten to close end of caterpillar and secure with a couple of backstitches.

FINISHING
Do not trim off the yarn tails (just leave them inside the caterpillar). If you wish to make the caterpillar bendable, cut a piece of wire a little longer than caterpillar. Using pliers, wrap each end of the wire back on itself for about 3mm (⅛in) to make a rounded end. Fold body in half lengthways, enclosing the wire and yarn tails inside, and sew seam using smooth black yarn. No stuffing is necessary because the yarn is fluffy enough to fill out the shape of the caterpillar.

The arrival of the woolly bear (or woolly worm) caterpillar coincides with the end of summer and beginning of autumn when sunflowers are blooming. There are woolly bear festivals in different parts of the United States. The adult form of this caterpillar is the tiger moth.

The synthetic fringed yarn used to make the caterpillars will add texture and shine to a display of sunflowers and leaves – as well as a touch of fun.

Robin

directory view page 47

Yarn: Aran-weight wool in reddish orange (A), grey (B), brown tweed (C) and pale gold (D)

Extras: Two stitch holders (or spare needles); set of four double-pointed needles (dpn) for working head; two 8mm (³/₈in) round black beads for eyes; black sewing thread and needle; ecru cotton embroidery thread and suitable sharp needle; polyester toy stuffing (optional)

METHOD

BELLY

Using A, cast on 7 sts.

Row 1 (RS): Knit.

Row 2 & all WS rows: Purl.

Row 3: K1, m1, k5, m1, k1. (9 sts)

Row 5: [K1, m1] twice, k5, [m1, k1] twice. (13 sts)

Row 7: [K1, m1] 3 times, k7, [m1, k1] 3 times. (19 sts)

Row 9: K1, m1, k to last st, m1, k1. (21 sts)

Row 11: Knit.

Row 13: K1, m1, k to last st, m1, k1. (23 sts)

Row 15: Knit.

Row 17: K1, m1, k to last st, m1, k1. (25 sts)

Row 19: Knit.

Row 21: K23 to last 2 sts, w&t, p21 to last 2 sts, w&t, k20 to last 3 sts, w&t, p19 to last 3 sts, w&t, k22 to end.

Row 23: Knit all sts.

Row 25: As row 21.

Row 27: K17 to last 8 sts, k2tog, w&t, slip first st, p9 to last 8 sts, p2tog, w&t, slip first st, k9 to last 7 sts, k2tog, w&t, slip first st, p9 to last 7 sts, p2tog, w&t, slip first st, k9 to last 6 sts, k2tog, w&t, slip first st, p9 to last 6 sts, p2tog, p to end. (19 sts)

Row 28 (RS): K2tog, k to last 2 sts, k2tog. (17 sts)

Row 30: K2tog, k1, k2tog, k to last 5 sts, k2tog, k1, k2tog. (13 sts)

Row 32: K2tog, k1, k2tog, k3, k2tog, k1, k2tog. (9 sts)

Row 33: Purl.

Break off yarn and slip remaining 9 sts on to stitch holder.

TAIL AND BACK

Using B, cast on 19 sts.

Row 1 (RS): K2, p3, k9, p3, k2.

Rows 2, 4, 6, 8, 10 & 12: K the k sts and p the p sts as they appear.

Row 3: K2, p3, k3, cdd, k3, p3, k2. (17 sts)

Row 5: K2, p3, k2, cdd, k2, p3, k2. (15 sts)

Row 7: K2, p3, k1, cdd, k1, p3, k2. (13 sts)

Row 9: K2, p1, p2tog, k3, p2tog, p1, k2. (11 sts)

Row 11: K2, p2, k3, p2, k2.

Row 13: Ssk, p2tog, k3, p2tog, k2tog. (7 sts)

Row 14: Purl. Place marker on this WS row.

Row 15: Knit.

Row 16 & all following WS rows: Purl.

Row 17: K1, m1, k5, m1, k1. (9 sts)

Row 19: Knit.

Row 21: K1, m1, k7, m1, k1. (11 sts)

Row 23: Knit.

Row 25: K1, m1, k9, m1, k1. (13 sts)

Row 27: K1, m1, k11, m1, k1. (15 sts)

Row 29: K1, m1, k13, m1, k1. (17 sts)

Row 31: K1, m1, k15, m1, k1. (19 sts)

Row 33: K1, m1, k17, m1, k1. (21 sts)

Rows 35, 37 & 39: Knit.

Row 40: Purl.

Shape right side of neck as follows:

Row 41: K7, slip rem 14 sts on to second stitch holder.

Continue on first 7 sts only as follows:

Rows 42, 44, 46 & 48: Purl.

Row 43: K5, k2tog. (6 sts)

Row 45: K2tog, k2, k2tog. (4 sts)

Row 47: [K2tog] twice. (2 sts)

Row 49: K2tog. (1 st)

Break off yarn and pass through remaining stitch.

Shape left side of neck as follows:

Slip last 7 sts from second stitch holder on to left needle, leaving centre 7 sts on holder.

Row 41: K7.

Rows 42 & 44: Purl.

Row 43: K2tog, k5. (6 sts)

Rows 45–49: As for right side of neck.

Break off yarn and pass through remaining stitch.

This is an American robin, not a European robin. Although both have reddish-orange breasts, the American species is a member of the thrush family, while the European robin belongs to the flycatcher family.

Size: Approx. 23cm (9in) long, using 4mm needles

ASSEMBLING BODY

Using B, sew the two pieces together, attaching belly at each end of marked row just above tail section (leave cast-on edge of belly unattached to allow for stuffing later). Ease the side edges so that last row of belly meets top of neck shaping.

HEAD

Note: The head is worked on a set of four dpn, working in rounds for 6 rounds, then working back and forth in rows to shape the head (there will be a seam at centre front of head). Where necessary, slip sts from one dpn to another to adjust the number of stitches on each needle. Always slip the stitches purlwise.

Using C, begin at upper body section as follows: using first dpn, pick up and knit 5 sts from right side of neck, knit 7 sts from second stitch holder; using second dpn, pick up and knit 5 sts from left side of neck; using third dpn, knit across belly sts from first stitch holder, working 2 sts together at centre to make 8 sts from 9 sts on holder. (25 sts)

Rounds 1–5: Knit.

Round 6: K4, k2tog, k5, k2tog, k to end. (23 sts)

Break off C and redistribute sts on needles as follows: slip last 4 sts of round 6 on to first dpn, then first 3 sts of round 6; slip next 9 sts on to second dpn; slip rem 7 sts on to third dpn. (23 sts)

Rejoin C between first and third dpn and work in rows, beginning and ending each row at centre front of neck as follows:

Row 1 (RS): Knit to end.

Row 2: Purl to end.

Begin short-row shaping for top of head as follows:

K22 to last st, turn.
P21 to last st, turn.
K20 to last 2 sts, turn.
P19 to last 2 sts, turn.
K18 to last 3 sts, turn.
P17 to last 3 sts, turn.

Continue in this way for eight more rows, until 7 sts remain unworked at each end, ending with a purl row.

Now join centre sts on second dpn to unworked sts on first and third dpn, beginning with sts on second dpn where you just left off as follows:

Row 1 (RS): Slip 1, k7, slip 1 st from next dpn on to centre dpn, k2tog, turn.

Row 2: Slip 1, p7, slip 1 st from next dpn on to centre dpn, p2tog, turn.

Repeat rows 1–2 six more times, ending with a WS row. (9 sts rem on centre dpn)

Break off C and join D to work beak.

BEAK

Row 1 (RS): Knit. (9 sts)

Row 2: Purl.

Row 3: K1, k2tog, k3, k2tog, k1. (7 sts)

Row 4: Purl.

Row 5: K2, cdd, k2. (5 sts)

Row 6: P2tog, p1, p2tog. (3 sts)

Row 7: Cdd. (1 st)

Break off yarn and pass through remaining stitch, leaving 15cm (6in) tail for seaming beak.

WINGS (make 2)

Using B, cast on 2 sts.

Row 1 (RS): Knit.

Row 2: Purl.

Row 3: Kfb, m1, kfb. (5 sts)

Row 4: P1, k1, p1, k1, p1.

Row 5: K1, m1, p1, k1, p1, m1, k1. (7 sts)

Row 6: P2, k1, p1, k1, p2.

Row 7: K1, m1, [k1, p1] twice, k1, m1, k1. (9 sts)

Rows 8, 10 & 12: [P1, k1] 4 times, p1.

Rows 9 & 11: [K1, p1] 4 times, k1.

Row 13: K1, m1, [p1, k1] 3 times, p1, m1, k1. (11 sts)

Rows 14, 16, 18 & 20: [K1, p1] 5 times, k1.

Rows 15, 17 & 19: [P1, k1] 5 times, p1.

Row 21: K2tog, [p1, k1] 3 times, p1, k2tog. (9 sts)

Row 22: K2tog, [p1, k1] twice, p1, k2tog. (7 sts)

Row 23: K2tog, p1, k1, p1, k2tog. (5 sts)

Cast off in k and p as set.

FINISHING

Using tails of yarn, sew top of wings to body. Stuff robin with scraps of yarn B or polyester toy stuffing, working stuffing in from lower opening at tail and upper opening at head. Any holes at top of head where short rows were worked may be closed by stitching firmly with yarn C. Join neck and beak seam. Close tail opening. Using sewing thread, sew a bead at each side of head for eyes. Using embroidery thread, stitch a few small lines above and below each bead to form small crescent shapes.

CROCHET DESIGNS

SEE ALSO

Notes on crochet, pages 16–21

Additional know-how, pages 22–23

Felting, pages 24–25

Embellishment, pages 26–27

Starburst

directory view page 35

Yarn: Aran-weight wool in orange (A), fuchsia (B) and gold (C)
Size: Approx. 15cm (6in) diameter, using 5mm hook

METHOD

CENTRE DISC

Using A, ch 5 and join with sl st to form a ring. Work in a spiral as follows:

Round 1: 7 dc in ring.

Round 2: 2 dc in each dc. (14 sts)

Round 3: [2 dc in next dc, 1 dc in next dc] 7 times. (21 sts)

Fasten off with sl st in next dc.

OUTER PETALS

Join B with sl st in back loop of any dc on round 3.

Round 4: [Ch 7, sk first ch, 1 dc in each of next 6 ch, sl st in back loop of next dc on round 3] 21 times. (21 petals)

Fasten off.

INNER PETALS

Join C with sl st in front loop of any dc on round 3.

Round 5: [Ch 5, sl st in front loop of next dc on round 3] 21 times. (21 petals)

Fasten off.

The flower has been left unblocked in order to retain the natural twist of the petals.

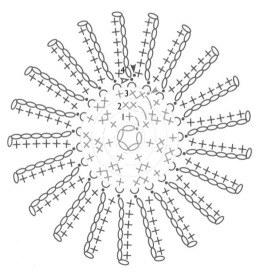

Centre disc and outer petals

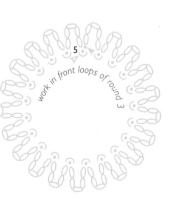

Inner petals

33 *Little Gem*
directory view pages 35 & 42

Yarn: Aran-weight wool in disc colour (A) and petal colour (B)
Size: Approx. 9cm (3¹/₂in) diameter, using 4.5mm hook

METHOD
CENTRE DISC
Using A, ch 5 and join with sl st to form a ring. Work in a spiral as follows:
Round 1: 9 dc in ring.
Round 2: 2 dc in each dc. (18 sts)
Fasten off with sl st in next dc.

PETALS
Join B with sl st to any dc on round 2.
Round 3: [Ch 3, 2 dtr in next dc, ch 3, sl st in next dc] 9 times. (9 petals)
Fasten off.

Felted variation with French knot embroidery.

34 *Picot Star*
directory view pages 36, 39, 43 & 46

Yarn: Aran-weight wool in disc colour (A) and petal colour (C); fringed yarn in toning colour (B) (optional)
Size: Approx. 11.5cm (4¹/₂in) diameter, using 4.5mm hook

METHOD
Note: Ch-3 picot = ch 3, sl st in 3rd ch from hook.

CENTRE DISC
Using A, ch 5 and join with sl st to form a ring. Work in a spiral as follows:
Round 1: 9 dc in ring.
Round 2: 2 dc in each dc. (18 sts)
Continue using A or change to B for next round.
Round 3: [2 dc in next dc, 1 dc in next dc] 9 times. (27 sts)
Fasten off with sl st in next dc.

PETALS
Join C with sl st to any dc on round 3.
Round 4: [Ch 2, (1 tr, 1 dtr) in next dc, ch-3 picot, (1 dtr, 1 tr) in next dc, ch 2, sl st in next dc] 9 times. (9 petals)
Fasten off.

Round 3 has been worked in a fringed yarn. Do not steam if using synthetic yarn so that the flower remains fluffy and lively.

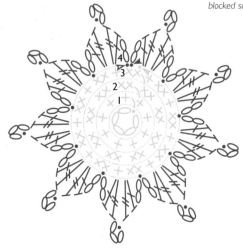

This flower in two colours has been blocked so that the petals lie flat.

Moulin Rouge
directory view page 48

Yarn: Aran-weight cotton in dark brown (A); fringed yarn in copper (B); aran-weight wool in maroon (C)
Size: Approx. 18cm (7in) diameter; using 4.5mm hook

METHOD
CENTRE DISC
Using A, ch 5 and join with sl st to form a ring. Work in a spiral as follows:
Round 1: 9 dc in ring.
Round 2: 2 dc in each dc. (18 sts)
Round 3: [2 dc in next dc, 1 dc in next dc] 9 times. (27 sts)
Round 4: [2 dc in next dc, 1 dc in each of next 2 dc] 9 times. (36 sts)
Round 5: [2 dc in next dc, 1 dc in each of next 3 dc] 9 times. (45 sts)
Fasten off A and join B in same place.
Round 6: [2 dc in next dc, 1 dc in each of next 4 dc] 9 times. (54 sts)
Round 7: [2 dc in next dc, 1 dc in each of next 5 dc] 9 times. (63 sts)
Fasten off B and rejoin A in same place to work back of disc.
Round 8: [1 dc in each of next 6 dc, sk next dc] 9 times. (54 sts)
Round 9: [1 dc in each of next 5 dc, sk next dc] 9 times. (45 sts)
Round 10: [1 dc in each of next 4 dc, sk next dc] 9 times. (36 sts)
Round 11: [1 dc in each of next 3 dc, sk next dc] 9 times. (27 sts)
Round 12: [1 dc in each of next 2 dc, sk next dc] 9 times. (18 sts)
Round 13: [1 dc in next dc, sk next dc] 9 times. (9 sts)
Fasten off with sl st in next dc, leaving tail of yarn for sewing up.

PETALS (make 16)
Using C, ch 8.
Row 1: Sk first ch, sl st in next ch, 1 dc in each of next 3 ch, 1 htr in each of next 2 ch, 3 dc in last chain (base of petal). Continuing along other side of chain, 1 htr in each of next 2 ch, 1 dc in each of next 3 ch.
Fasten off with sl st at top of petal.

FINISHING
Stuff centre disc with scraps of yarn A (or similar colour), then sew opening closed with tail of yarn. Using C, sew base of petals evenly spaced around back of disc.

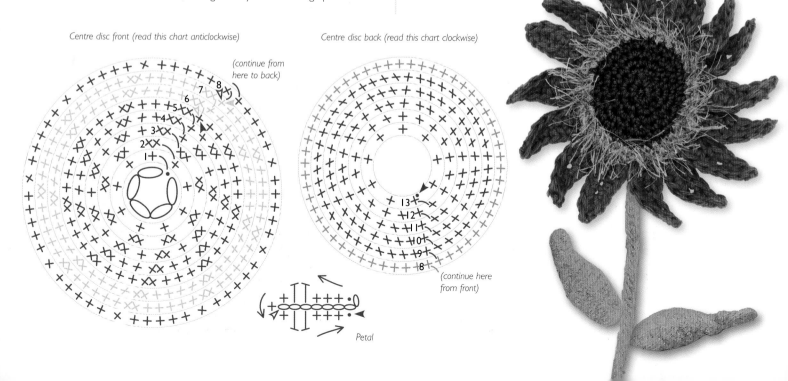

Centre disc front (read this chart anticlockwise)

(continue from here to back)

Centre disc back (read this chart clockwise)

(continue here from front)

Petal

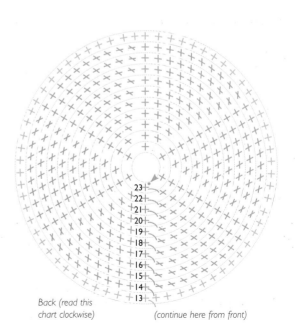

36 *Big Teddy Bear*

directory view page 39

Yarn: DK-weight cotton in green (A) and yellow (C); fringed yarn in yellow (B)
Size: Approx. 11.5cm (4¹/₂in) diameter, using 4mm hook

METHOD

Using A, ch 5 and join with sl st to form a ring. Work in a spiral as follows:
Round 1: 6 dc in ring.
Round 2: 2 dc in each dc. (12 sts)
Round 3: [2 dc in next dc, 1 dc in next dc] 6 times. (18 sts)
Fasten off A and join B in same place.
Round 4: [2 dc in next dc, 1 dc in each of next 2 dc] 6 times. (24 sts)
Round 5: [2 dc in next dc, 1 dc in each of next 3 dc] 6 times. (30 sts)
Round 6: [2 dc in next dc, 1 dc in each of next 4 dc] 6 times. (36 sts)
Round 7: [2 dc in next dc, 1 dc in each of next 5 dc] 6 times. (42 sts)
Round 8: [2 dc in next dc, 1 dc in each of next 6 dc] 6 times. (48 sts)
Round 9: [2 dc in next dc, 1 dc in each of next 7 dc] 6 times. (54 sts)
Round 10: [2 dc in next dc, 1 dc in each of next 8 dc] 6 times. (60 sts)
Round 11: [2 dc in next dc, 1 dc in each of next 9 dc] 6 times. (66 sts)
Round 12: [2 dc in next dc, 1 dc in each of next 10 dc] 6 times. (72 sts)
Fasten off B and join C in same place to work back of flower.
Round 13: [1 dc in each of next 11 dc, sk next dc] 6 times. (66 sts)
Round 14: [1 dc in each of next 10 dc, sk next dc] 6 times. (60 sts)
Round 15: [1 dc in each of next 9 dc, sk next dc] 6 times. (54 sts)

Round 16: [1 dc in each of next 8 dc, sk next dc] 6 times. (48 sts)
Round 17: [1 dc in each of next 7 dc, sk next dc] 6 times. (42 sts)
Round 18: [1 dc in each of next 6 dc, sk next dc] 6 times. (36 sts)
Round 19: [1 dc in each of next 5 dc, sk next dc] 6 times. (30 sts)
Round 20: [1 dc in each of next 4 dc, sk next dc] 6 times. (24 sts)
Round 21: [1 dc in each of next 3 dc, sk next dc] 6 times. (18 sts)
Round 22: [1 dc in each of next 2 dc, sk next dc] 6 times. (12 sts)
Round 23: [1 dc in next dc, sk next dc] 6 times. (6 sts)
Fasten off with sl st in next dc, leaving tail of yarn for sewing up.

FINISHING

Stuff sunflower with scraps of yarn B (or similar colour), then sew opening closed with tail of yarn.

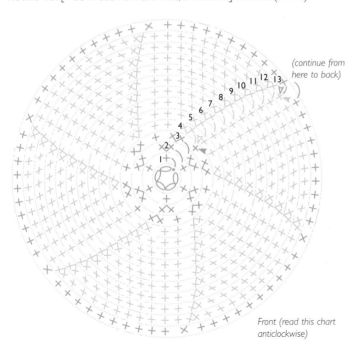

(continue from here to back)

Front (read this chart anticlockwise)

Back (read this chart clockwise)

(continue here from front)

37 *Raspberry Ruffle*

directory view pages 40 & 43

Yarn: DK-weight wool/cotton blend in brown (A), pink (B) and green (C)
Size: Approx. 11.5cm (4½in) diameter with petals spread open, using 4mm hook

METHOD

CENTRE DISC

Using A, ch 5 and join with sl st to form a ring. Work in a spiral as follows:
Round 1: 6 dc in ring.
Round 2: 2 dc in each dc. (12 sts)
Round 3: [2 dc in next dc, 1 dc in next dc] 6 times. (18 sts)
Round 4: [2 dc in next dc, 1 dc in each of next 2 dc] 6 times. (24 sts)
Round 5: [2 dc in next dc, 1 dc in each of next 3 dc] 6 times. (30 sts)
Fasten off with sl st in next dc.

PETALS

Join B with sl st to any dc on round 5.
Round 6: [Ch 6, sl st in 2nd ch from hook, 1 dc in next ch, 1 htr in next ch, 2 tr in each of next 2 ch (petal made); sk next dc on round 5 and attach petal with 1 dc in next dc] 15 times. (15 petals)
Fasten off.

If you leave the flower unblocked, the petals will curl around the centre disc and form a double ruffle.

RUFFLE BORDER

Join C with sl st to any empty dc on round 5 and work in front of petals as follows:
Round 7: [Ch 3, sl st in 2nd ch from hook, 1 dc in next ch (ruffle made), sl st in next empty dc on round 5] 15 times. (15 ruffles)
Fasten off.

Felted variation worked in wool yarn with French knot embroidery.

For a flower in full bloom, block the sunflower with the petals pinned out.

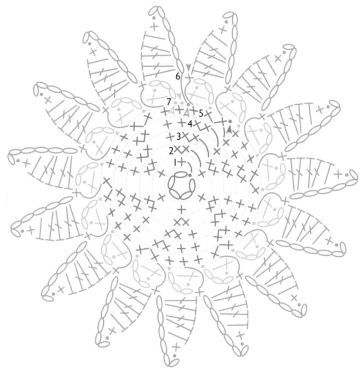

38 *Sunbright*
directory view page 45

Yarn: Aran-weight wool in fuchsia (A) and orange (B)
Size: Approx. 10cm (4in) diameter; using 5mm hook

You can vary the size of the petals by increasing the number of chains.

METHOD
CENTRE DISC
Using A, ch 5 and join with sl st to form a ring.
Work in a spiral as follows:
Round 1: 7 dc in ring.
Round 2: 2 dc in each dc. (14 sts)
Round 3: [2 dc in next dc, 1 dc in next dc] 7 times. (21 sts)
Fasten off with sl st in next dc.

PETALS
Join B with sl st to any dc on round 3.
Round 4: [Ch 7, sl st in next dc] 21 times. (21 petals)
Fasten off.

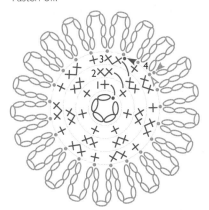

39 *Sunburst*
directory view page 46

Yarn: Aran-weight wool in fuchsia (A) and gold (B)
Size: Approx. 15cm (6in) diameter; using 5mm hook

METHOD
CENTRE DISC
Using A, ch 5 and join with sl st to form a ring. Work in a spiral as follows:
Round 1: 7 dc in ring.
Round 2: 2 dc in each dc. (14 sts)
Round 3: [2 dc in next dc, 1 dc in next dc] 7 times. (21 sts)
Fasten off with sl st in next dc.

PETALS
Join B with sl st to any dc on round 3.
Round 4: [Ch 7, sk first ch, 1 dc in each of next 6 ch, sl st in next dc] 21 times. (21 petals)
Fasten off.

Both Sunburst (right) and Sunbright (left) have been left unblocked in order to retain the natural twist of the petals.

40 *Flower Back and Stem*
directory view pages 43 & 48

Yarn: Aran-weight wool in green
Size: Cone approx. 4.5cm (1¾in) diameter; using 4.5mm hook; stem length as required

METHOD
CONE
Ch 5 and join with sl st to form a ring.
Work in a spiral as follows:
Round 1: 6 dc in ring.
Round 2: 2 dc in each dc. (12 sts)
Round 3: 1 dc in each dc.
Round 4: [2 dc in next dc, 1 dc in next dc] 6 times. (18 sts)
Round 5: 1 dc in each dc.
You can continue in this way, working an increase round followed by a plain round of dc, to fit the back of a larger sunflower.
Fasten off with sl st in next dc, leaving tail of yarn for sewing to flower.

STEM
Ch 15.
Row 1: Sk first ch (counts as 1 dc), 1 dc in each ch to end, turn. (15 sts)
Row 2: Ch 1, sk first dc, 1 dc in each of next 13 dc, 1 dc in ch 1, turn.
Row 3: As row 2.
Fasten off, leaving tail of yarn for sewing seam along length of stem. For a longer or shorter stem, begin with as many ch as required.

FINISHING
Fold stem in half lengthways and sew long edges together. Sew top of stem to back of cone. Stuff cone with scraps of yarn in matching colour and sew to back of sunflower.

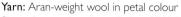

41 *Crochet Petals*
directory view pages 37 & 48

Yarn: Aran-weight wool in petal colour
Sizes: Approx. length: small 4cm (1½in); large 7.5cm (3in); square-ended 5.5cm (2¼in); all using 4.5mm hook

METHOD
SMALL
Ch 6.
Row 1: Sk first ch, sl st in next ch, 1 dc in next ch, 2 tr in next ch, 1 dc in next ch, 2 dc in last ch (base of petal). Continuing along other side of chain, 1 dc in next ch, 2 tr in next ch, 1 dc in next ch.
Fasten off with sl st at top of petal.

Small

LARGE
Ch 9.
Row 1: Sk first ch, sl st in next ch, 1 dc in next ch, 1 htr in next ch, 1 tr in next ch, 2 tr in next ch, 1 dtr in next ch, (1 dtr, 1 tr) in next ch, 5 tr in last ch (base of petal). Continuing along other side of chain, (1 tr, 1 dtr) in next ch, 1 dtr in next ch, 2 tr in next ch, 1 tr in next ch, 1 htr in next ch, 1 dc in next ch.
Fasten off with sl st at top of petal.

Large

SQUARE-ENDED
Ch 10.
Row 1: Sk first 3 ch, 1 tr in each of next 4 ch, 1 htr in next ch, 1 dc in next ch, sl st in last ch, ch 2 (top of petal). Continuing along other side of chain, sl st in next ch, 1 dc in next ch, 1 htr in next ch, 1 tr in each of next 4 ch, 1 tr in base of skipped ch 3 at beg of row.
Fasten off.

Square-ended

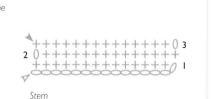

Cone

Stem

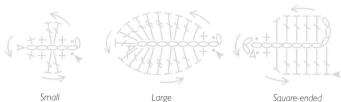

Small

Large

Square-ended

42 *Teardrop and Toothed Leaves*
directory view pages 35, 36, 38, 42, 44, 46, 47, 48 & 49

Yarn: Aran-weight wool in green
Sizes: Approx. length: small 4cm (1½in); medium 6.5cm (2½in); large 8.5cm (3¼in); extra large 13.5cm (5¼in); excluding picot edges and all using 4.5mm hook

METHOD

SMALL
Ch 6.
Row 1: Sk first ch, sl st in next ch, 1 dc in next ch, 2 tr in next ch, 1 dc in next ch, 2 dc in last ch (base of leaf). Continuing along other side of chain, 1 dc in next ch, 2 tr in next ch, 1 dc in next ch.
Fasten off with sl st at top of leaf.

MEDIUM
Ch 8.
Row 1: Sk first ch, sl st in next ch, 1 dc in each of next 2 ch, (1 htr, 1 tr) in next ch, 2 tr in next ch, 2 dtr in next ch, 5 tr in last ch (base of leaf). Continuing along other side of chain, 2 dtr in next ch, 2 tr in next ch, (1 tr, 1 htr) in next ch, 1 dc in each of next 2 ch.
Fasten off with sl st at top of leaf.

LARGE
Ch 9.
Row 1: Sk first ch, sl st in next ch, 1 dc in each of next 2 ch, 1 htr in next ch, 2 tr in next ch, (1 tr, 1 dtr) in next ch, 2 dtr in next ch, 7 tr in last ch (base of leaf). Continuing along other side of chain, 2 dtr in next ch, (1 dtr, 1 tr) in next ch, 2 tr in next ch, 1 htr in next ch, 1 dc in each of next 2 ch, sl st in next ch.

Small

Medium

Large

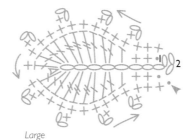

Extra large

Fasten off or add picot edge as follows:
Row 2: Ch 2, [1 dc in each of next 3 sts, ch 2, 1 dc in second ch from hook] 8 times, 1 dc in each of next 3 sts.
Fasten off with sl st at top of leaf.

EXTRA LARGE
Ch 12.
Row 1: Sk first ch, sl st in next ch, (1 dc, 1 htr) in next ch, 2 tr in next ch, (1 tr, 1 dtr) in next ch, 2 dtr in next ch, 1 dtr in each of next 2 ch, 2 ttr in each of next 3 ch, 7 ttr in last ch (base of leaf). Continuing along other side of chain, 2 ttr in each of next 3 ch, 1 dtr in each of next 2 ch, 2 dtr in next ch, (1 dtr, 1 tr) in next ch, 2 tr in next ch, (1 htr, 1 dc) in next ch, sl st in next ch.
Fasten off or add picot edge as follows:
Row 2: Ch 2, sk first sl st, [1 dc in each of next 3 sts, ch 2, 1 dc in second ch from hook] 3 times, [1 dc in each of next 3 sts, ch 3, sk first ch from hook, 1 dc in each of next 2 ch] 6 times, [1 dc in each of next 3 sts, ch 2, 1 dc in second ch from hook] 3 times, 1 dc in each of next 3 sts.
Fasten off with sl st at top of leaf.

Large with picot edge

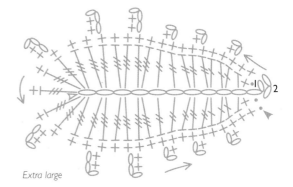

Extra large with picot edge

Small

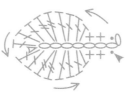

Medium

Large

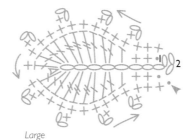

Extra large

43 *Purple Passion*

directory view pages 42 & 43

Yarn: Aran-weight wool in dusky pink (A), light pink (B), orange (C), purple (D) and green (E)
Size: Approx. 22cm (8¾in) diameter, using 4.5mm hook

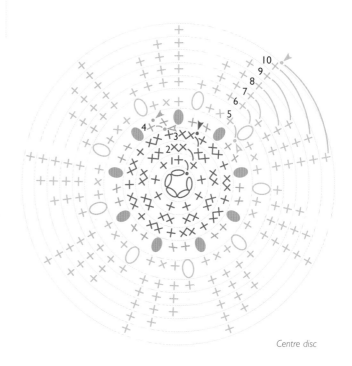

METHOD

Note: M4trB = make 4-tr bobble; M5dtrB = make 5-dtr bobble (see page 21).

CENTRE DISC

Using A, ch 5 and join with sl st to form a ring. Work in a spiral as follows:
Round 1: 9 dc in ring.
Round 2: 2 dc in each dc. (18 sts)
Round 3: [2 dc in next dc, 1 dc in next dc] 9 times. (27 sts)
Fasten off A with sl st in next dc and join B with sl st to any dc on round 3.
Round 4: [1 dc in next dc, M4trB in next dc, 1 dc in next dc] 9 times.
Fasten off B with sl st in next dc and join C with sl st to dc at right of any bobble on round 4.
Round 5: [1 dc in next st (the tr4tog of bobble), 1 dc in ch closing bobble, 1 dc in next dc, M5dtrB in next dc] 9 times.
Continue in C to work back of disc as follows:
Round 6: [1 dc in each of next 3 dc, 1 dc in ch closing bobble] 9 times. (36 sts)
Round 7: [1 dc in each of next 3 dc, sk next dc] 9 times. (27 sts)
Round 8: 1 dc in each dc.
Round 9: [1 dc in each of next 2 dc, sk next dc] 9 times. (18 sts)

Round 10: [1 dc in next dc, sk next dc] 9 times. (9 sts) Fasten off with sl st in next dc, leaving tail of yarn for sewing up.

PETALS AND STEM

Using D, make nine large petals (see page 80). Using E, make a flower back and stem (see page 80).

FINISHING

Stuff centre disc with scraps of yarn A (or similar colour), then sew opening closed with tail of yarn. Using E (or similar colour), stuff cone at top of stem and sew to back of centre disc. Using D, sew base of petals evenly spaced around back of disc.

Centre disc

44 *Ruby Harvest*
directory view page 48

Yarn: Aran-weight wool in brown (A), red (B), pale gold (C) and chartreuse (D)
Size: Approx. 13.5cm (5¹/₄in) diameter; using 4.5mm hook

METHOD
Note: M5trB = make 5-tr bobble (see page 21).

CENTRE DISC
Using A, ch 5 and join with sl st to form a ring. Work in a spiral as follows:
Round 1: 7 dc in ring.
Round 2: 2 dc in each dc. (14 sts)
Round 3: [2 dc in next dc, 1 dc in next dc] 7 times. (21 sts)
Fasten off A with sl st in next dc and join B with sl st to any dc on round 3.
Round 4: [1 dc in next dc, M5trB in next dc, 1 dc in next dc] 7 times.
Round 5: 1 dc in each dc and 1 dc in each ch closing bobble. (21 sts)
Round 6: 1 dc in each dc.
Round 7: [1 dc in each of next 2 dc, sk next dc] 7 times. (14 sts)
Round 8: 1 dc in each dc.
Round 9: [1 dc in next dc, sk next dc] 7 times. (7 sts)
Fasten off with sl st in next dc, leaving tail of yarn for sewing up.

PETALS, STEM AND LEAVES
Using C, make fourteen small petals (see page 80). Using D, make a flower back and stem (see page 80) and three small leaves (see page 81).

FINISHING
Stuff centre disc with scraps of yarn A (or similar colour), then sew opening closed with tail of yarn. Using D (or similar colour), stuff cone at top of stem and sew to back of centre disc. Using C, sew base of seven petals evenly spaced around back of disc. Sew base of remaining seven petals around disc, positioning them behind the spaces between the first seven petals. Using D, sew base of leaves around top of stem.

After attaching the flower back and stem to the back of the centre disc, sew on the petals and leaves in overlapping layers.

Centre disc

45 Openwork Star

directory view page 44

Yarn: Aran-weight wool in gold (A), fuchsia (B) and orange (C)
Size: Approx. 15cm (6in) diameter, using 5mm hook

METHOD
CENTRE DISC
Using A, ch 5 and join with sl st to form a ring. Work in a spiral as follows:
Round 1: 7 dc in ring.
Round 2: 2 dc in each dc. (14 sts)
Fasten off A with sl st in next dc and join B with sl st to any dc on round 2.
Round 3: [2 dc in next dc, 1 dc in next dc] 7 times. (21 sts)
Fasten off B with sl st in next dc and join C with sl st to any dc on round 3.
Round 4: [2 dc in next dc, 1 dc in each of next 2 dc] 6 times, 1 dc in each of next 3 dc. (27 sts)

PETALS
Continue using C.
Round 5: [Ch 7, sk first ch, sl st in next ch, 1 dc in next ch, 1 htr in next ch, 1 tr in each of next 2 ch (petal made); sk last ch, sk 2 dc on round 4 and attach petal with 1 dc in next dc] 9 times. (9 petals)
Fasten off.

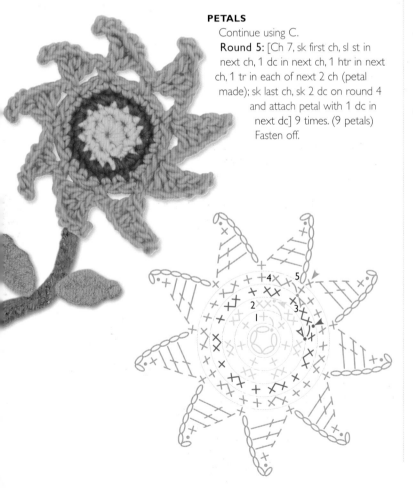

46 Sea Anemone

directory view page 47

Yarn: Aran-weight wool in chartreuse (A), pink (B) and maroon (C)
Size: Approx. 10cm (4in) diameter, using 4.5mm hook

METHOD
CENTRE DISC
Using A, ch 5 and join with sl st to form a ring. Work in a spiral as follows:
Round 1: 7 dc in ring.
Round 2: 2 dc in each dc. (14 sts)
Fasten off with sl st in next dc.

OUTER PETALS
Join B with sl st in back loop of any dc on round 2.
Round 3: [Ch 6, sk first ch, 1 dc in next ch, 1 htr in next ch, 1 tr in next ch, 1 dtr in next ch, 1 ttr in next ch, sl st in back loop of next dc on round 2] 14 times. (14 petals)
Fasten off.

INNER PETALS
Join C with sl st in front loop of any dc on round 2.
Round 4: [Ch 5, sl st in front loop of next dc on round 2] 14 times. (14 petals)
Fasten off.

The petals are designed to curl up. Do not block or the curl will disappear.

47 *Small Bud*
directory view page 40

Yarn: Aran-weight wool in chartreuse (A) and pale gold (B) **Size:** Approx. 6.5cm (2¹⁄₂in) diameter, using 4.5mm hook

METHOD
CENTRE DISC
Using A, ch 5 and join with sl st to form a ring. Work in a spiral as follows:
Round 1: 7 dc in ring.
Round 2: 2 dc in each dc. (14 sts)
Round 3: [2 dc in next dc, 1 dc in next dc] 7 times. (21 sts)
Fasten off with sl st in next dc.

PETALS
Join B with sl st to any dc on round 3.
Round 4: [(1 tr, 2 dtr, 1 tr) in next dc, sl st in each of next 2 dc] 6 times, (1 tr, 2 dtr, 1 tr) in next dc, sl st in next dc. (7 petals)
Fasten off with sl st in next dc.

48 *Large Bud*
directory view page 40

Yarn: Aran-weight wool in rust (A) and chartreuse (B)
Size: Approx. 8cm (3¹⁄₄in) diameter, using 4.5mm hook

METHOD
Note: M6dtrB = make 6-dtr bobble (see page 21).

CENTRE DISC
Using A, ch 5 and join with sl st to form a ring. Work in a spiral as follows:
Round 1: 7 dc in ring.
Round 2: 2 dc in each dc. (14 sts)
Round 3: [2 dc in next dc, 1 dc in next dc] 7 times. (21 sts)
Fasten off with sl st in next dc.

INNER PETALS
Join B with sl st in front loop of any dc on round 3.
Round 4: Ch 3, (1 dtr, 1 tr) in same front loop at base of ch 3, [sl st in front loop of each of next 2 dc, (1 tr, 1 dtr, 1 tr) in front loop of next dc] 6 times, sl st in front loop of each of next 2 dc. (7 petals)

OUTER PETALS
Work outer petals in back loops of dc on round 3 as follows:
Round 5: Sl st in back loop of next dc (which contains an inner petal), [M6dtrB over back loops of next 2 dc, sl st in back loop of next dc] 7 times. (7 petals)
Fasten off. Push a finger into each bobble from RS of work, so that fullness of bobble goes outwards from centre to look like a budding petal.

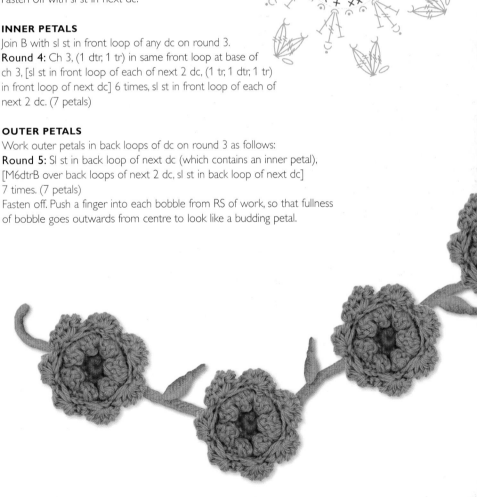

Tweed Giant
directory view pages 40 & 47

Yarn: Aran-weight tweed wool in chartreuse (A) (optional), brown (B), green (C) and orange or pale yellow (D)
Size: Approx. 25cm (10in) diameter with petals spread open, using 4.5mm hook

METHOD

CENTRE DISC AND STEM

Using A for two-colour centre or B for single-colour centre, ch 4 and join with sl st to form a ring. Work in a spiral as follows:

Round 1: 5 dc in ring.
Round 2: 2 dc in each dc. (10 sts)
Round 3: [2 dc in next dc, 1 dc in next dc] 5 times. (15 sts)
Round 4: [2 dc in next dc, 1 dc in each of next 2 dc] 5 times. (20 sts)
Round 5: [2 dc in next dc, 1 dc in each of next 3 dc] 5 times. (25 sts)
Round 6: [2 dc in next dc, 1 dc in each of next 4 dc] 5 times. (30 sts)
If working two-colour centre, fasten off A and join B in same place.
Round 7: [2 dc in next dc, 1 dc in each of next 5 dc] 5 times. (35 sts)
Round 8: [2 dc in next dc, 1 dc in each of next 6 dc] 5 times. (40 sts)
Round 9: 1 dc in each dc.
Round 10: As round 9.
Round 11: [Sk next dc, 1 dc in each of next 4 dc] 8 times. (32 sts).
Round 12: [Sk next dc, 1 dc in each of next 3 dc] 8 times. (24 sts).
Fasten off B and join C in same place.

Round 13: 1 dc in each dc.
Round 14: As round 13.
Round 15: [Sk next dc, 1 dc in each of next 2 dc] 8 times. (16 sts)
Round 16: 1 dc in each dc.
Round 17: [Sk next dc, 1 dc in next dc] 8 times. (8 sts)
Stuff centre disc with scraps of yarn in matching colour.
Round 18: [Sk next dc, 1 dc in each of next 3 dc] twice. (6 sts)
Continue by working 1 dc in each dc, forming a spiral tube on these 6 sts to length of stem required, then fasten off with sl st in next dc.

LARGE PETALS (make 11)

Using D, ch 10.
Row 1: Sk first ch, sl st in next ch, 1 dc in each of next 3 ch, 1 tr in next ch, 2 tr in next ch, 2 dtr in next ch, 1 tr in next ch, 5 tr in last ch (base of petal). Continuing along other side of chain, 1 tr in next ch, 2 dtr in next ch, 2 tr in next ch, 1 tr in next ch, 1 dc in each of next 3 ch.
Fasten off with sl st at top of petal.

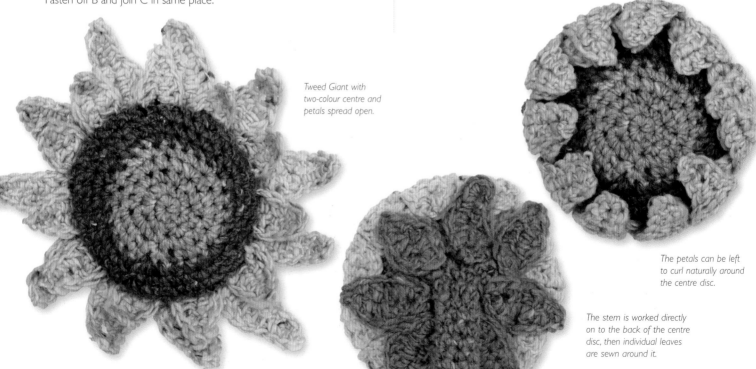

Tweed Giant with two-colour centre and petals spread open.

The petals can be left to curl naturally around the centre disc.

The stem is worked directly on to the back of the centre disc, then individual leaves are sewn around it.

SMALL PETALS (make 11)

Using D, ch 6.

Row 1: Sk first ch, 1 dc in each of next 2 ch, 1 tr in each of next 2 ch, 2 dc in last ch (base of petal). Continuing along other side of chain, 1 tr in each of next 2 ch, 1 dc in each of next 2 ch. Fasten off with sl st at top of petal.

LEAVES (make 7)

Using C, ch 7.

Row 1: Sk first ch, sl st in next ch, 1 dc in next ch, 1 tr in each of next 2 ch, 1 dc in next ch, 5 dc in last ch (base of leaf). Continuing along other side of chain, 1 dc in next ch, 1 tr in each of next 2 ch, 1 dc in next ch. Fasten off with sl st at top of leaf.

FINISHING

Using D, sew base of small petals evenly spaced around back of centre disc. Sew base of large petals around disc, positioning them behind the spaces between the small petals. Using C, sew base of leaves around top of stem.

Tweed Giant with single-colour centre.

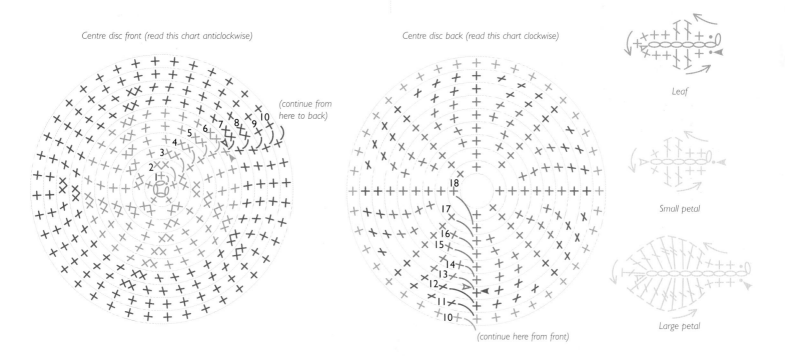

Centre disc front (read this chart anticlockwise)

(continue from here to back)

Centre disc back (read this chart clockwise)

(continue here from front)

Leaf

Small petal

Large petal

50 *Lace Sunbeam*
directory view page 34

Yarn: Aran-weight tweed wool in mid-brown (A) and dark brown (B); aran-weight wool in golden yellow (C)
Size: Approx. 25cm (10in) diameter, using 4.5mm hook

METHOD
Note: M5trB = make 5-tr bobble (see page 21).

CENTRE DISC
Using A, make a slip ring. Work in rounds as follows:
Round 1: Ch 1 (counts as 1 dc), 5 dc in ring, join with sl st in ch 1. (6 sts)
Pull starting yarn tail to tighten centre of ring.
Round 2: Ch 1, 1 dc in same place, 2 dc in each of next 5 dc, join with sl st in ch 1. (12 sts)
Round 3: Ch 1, [2 dc in next dc, 1 dc in next dc] 5 times, 2 dc in next dc, join with sl st in ch 1. (18 sts)
Round 4: Ch 1, [2 dc in next dc, 1 dc in each of next 2 dc] 5 times, 2 dc in next dc, 1 dc in next dc, join with sl st in ch 1. (24 sts)
Fasten off A and join B with sl st in ch 1 at beginning of round 4.
Round 5: Ch 1, [1 dc in each of next 2 dc, M5trB in next dc, 1 dc in next dc] 5 times, 1 dc in each of next 2 dc, M5trB in next dc, join with sl st in ch 1. (24 sts)

Fasten off B and join C with sl st in ch 1 at beginning of round 5.
Round 6: Ch 1, [1 dc in each of next 2 dc, 2 dc in ch closing bobble, 1 dc in next dc] 5 times, 1 dc in each of next 2 dc, 2 dc in ch closing bobble, join with sl st in ch 1. (30 sts)
Fasten off.

PETALS (make 12)
Using C and leaving tail of yarn for sewing petal to centre disc, ch 5.
Row 1 (RS): Sk first ch, 1 dc in each of next 4 ch, turn.
Row 2: Ch 1 (counts as 1 dc), 1 dc in first dc, 2 dc in each of next 3 dc, turn leaving ch 1 unworked. (8 sts)
Row 3: Ch 3, sk first dc, 1 tr in each of next 6 dc, 1 tr in ch 1, turn.
Row 4: Ch 1, sk first tr, 1 dc in each of next 6 tr, 1 dc in 3rd of ch 3, turn.
Row 5: Ch 1, sk first dc, [1 dc in next dc, sk next dc] 3 times, 1 dc in ch 1, turn.
Row 6: Ch 3 (counts as 1 tr), sk first dc, 1 tr in each of next 3 dc, turn leaving ch 1 unworked. (4 sts)
Row 7: Ch 1 (counts as 1 dc), sk first tr, 1 dc in next tr, sk next tr, 1 dc in 3rd of ch 3, turn. (3 sts)
Row 8: Ch 1, sk 2 dc, 1 dc in ch 1.
Fasten off.

FINISHING
Using tails of yarn, sew straight edge of six petals evenly spaced around edge of centre disc, aligning centre of each petal to a bobble. Sew base of remaining six petals around disc, positioning them behind the spaces between the first six petals.

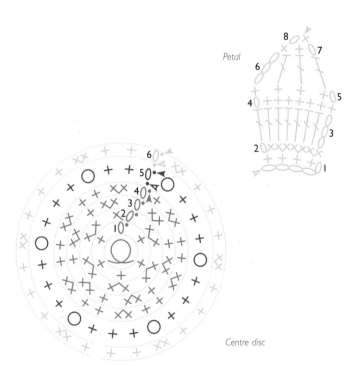

Petal

Centre disc

Bicolour Gem

51

directory view page 39

Yarn: Aran-weight wool in dark grey (A), chartreuse (B), pale gold (C) and orange (D)
Size: Approx. 15cm (6in) diameter, using 4.5mm hook

METHOD

LOWER CENTRE DISC

Using A, ch 5 and join with sl st to form a ring. Work in a spiral as follows:
Round 1: 7 dc in ring.
Round 2: 2 dc in each dc. (14 sts)
Round 3: [2 dc in next dc, 1 dc in next dc] 7 times. (21 sts)
Fasten off with sl st in next dc.

PETALS (make 7)

The petals are worked separately around centre disc. They are packed tightly and will ruffle slightly when finished. Each petal is worked back and forth in rows, beginning over 3 dc of round 3.
With RS facing, join B with sl st to any dc on round 3.
Row 1 (RS): Ch 1, 1 dc in each of next 2 dc, turn. (3 sts)
Row 2: Ch 3, 1 tr in dc below, 1 tr in next dc, 1 tr in ch 1, ch 3.
Fasten off with sl st in same dc on round 3 where B was joined.
With WS facing, join C with sl st to same dc on round 3 as last st of petal row 1.
Row 3: Working around edge of inner petal, 1 dc in side of row 1, 4 dc up side of ch 3, 1 dc in top of each of next 3 tr, 4 dc down side of ch 3, 1 dc in side of row 1, sl st in same dc on round 3 as first st of petal row 1.
Row 4: Turn to RS, sk first sl st, 1 dc in each of next 4 dc, ch 2, 2 tr in next dc, 1 dtr in next dc, 1 ttr in next dc, 1 dtr in next dc, 2 tr in next dc, ch 2, 1 dc in each of next 4 dc.
Fasten off with sl st in same dc on round 3 as last st of petal row 1.
Repeat to make next petal, beginning in next dc on round 3 of centre disc. Continue all around, making seven petals in total.

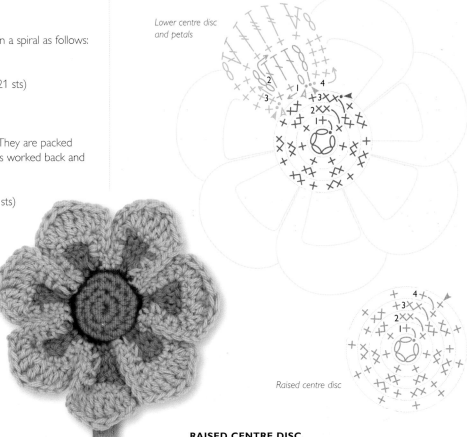

Lower centre disc and petals

Raised centre disc

RAISED CENTRE DISC

Using D, ch 5 and join with sl st to form a ring. Work in a spiral as follows:
Round 1: 7 dc in ring.
  Round 2: 2 dc in each dc. (14 sts)
    Round 3: [2 dc in next dc, 1 dc in next dc] 7 times. (21 sts)
    Round 4: [1 dc in next dc, sk next dc] 10 times, 1 dc in last dc. (11 sts)
  Cut D, leaving a long tail, and weave tail through last round. Pull to tighten and form a circle, then sew on to centre of flower.

Autumn Beauty
directory view page 36

Yarn: Aran-weight wool in golden yellow (A), rust (B), chartreuse (C) and orange (D)
Size: Approx. 26cm (10½in) diameter, using 4.5mm hook

METHOD
Note: M5trB = make 5-tr bobble (see page 21).

CENTRE DISC
Using A, ch 5 and join with sl st to form a ring. Work in a spiral as follows:
Round 1: 8 dc in ring.
Round 2: 2 dc in each dc. (16 sts)
Round 3: [2 dc in next dc, 1 dc in next dc] 8 times. (24 sts)
Round 4: [2 dc in next dc, 1 dc in each of next 2 dc] 7 times,
2 dc in each of next 2 dc, 1 dc in next dc. (33 sts)
Fasten off with sl st in next dc.

BOBBLE BORDER
Join B with sl st to any dc on round 4 and work in rounds as follows:
Round 5: Ch 1 (counts as 1 dc), [M5trB in next dc, 1 dc in each of next
2 dc] 10 times, M5trB in next dc, 1 dc in next dc, join with sl st in ch 1.
Fasten off B and join C with sl st in ch closing any bobble on round 5.
Round 6: Ch 1 (counts as 1 dc), 2 dc in same place, [sk next dc, M5trB in
next dc, 3 dc in ch closing next bobble] 10 times, sk next dc, M5trB in next
dc, join with sl st in ch 1.
Fasten off C and rejoin B with sl st in ch closing any
bobble on round 6.
Round 7: Ch 1 (counts as 1 dc), 1 dc in same
place, [1 dc in next dc, M5trB in next dc, 1 dc
in next dc, 2 dc in ch closing next bobble]
10 times, 1 dc in next dc, M5trB in next
dc, 1 dc in next dc, join with sl st in ch 1.
Fasten off.

PETALS (make 11)
Join D with sl st in ch closing any
bobble on round 7 and work each
petal back and forth in rows.
Row 1 (RS): 1 tr in next dc, sk next
dc, 5 dtr in next dc, 1 tr in next dc,
sl st in ch closing next bobble, turn.
Row 2: Ch 1 (counts as 1 dc),
sk first sl st, 1 dc in each of next
8 sts, turn. (9 sts)

Row 3: Ch 3, sk first dc, 1 tr in each
of next 7 dc, 1 tr in ch 1, turn.
Row 4: Ch 1, 1 dc in first tr, 1 htr
in next tr, 1 tr in next tr, 2 dtr in
next tr, 3 dtr in next tr, 2 dtr
in next tr, 1 tr in next tr, 1 htr
in next tr, 1 dc in 3rd of ch 3.
Fasten off.
Repeat to make next petal,
beginning in ch closing same
bobble as last st of row 1 of petal
just made. Continue all around,
making eleven petals in total.

53 *Aztec Gold*
directory view page 38

Yarn: Aran-weight wool in chartreuse (A), rust (B) and pale gold (C)
Size: Approx. 22cm (8¾in) diameter, using 4.5mm hook

METHOD

Note: This sunflower can be modified to have fewer petals by changing the number of stitches in round 1 of the centre disc. For example, this flower begins with 9 dc in round 1, then increases to 18, 27, 36, 45, 54, 63 and finally 72. If you were to begin with 6 dc, the increases would be to 12, 18, 24, 30, 36, 42 and finally 48. This would make a smaller sunflower with six petals.

CENTRE DISC

Using A, ch 7 and join with sl st to form a ring. Work in rounds as follows:
Round 1: Ch 1 (counts as 1 dc), 8 dc in ring, join with sl st in ch 1. (9 sts)
Round 2: Ch 1, 1 dc in st below, 2 dc in each of next 8 dc, join with sl st in ch 1. (18 sts)
Round 3: Ch 1, [2 dc in next dc, 1 dc in next dc] 8 times, 2 dc in next dc, join with sl st in ch 1. (27 sts)

Round 4: Ch 1, [2 dc in next dc, 1 dc in each of next 2 dc] 8 times, 2 dc in next dc, 1 dc in next dc, join with sl st in ch 1. (36 sts)
Round 5: Ch 1, [2 dc in next dc, 1 dc in each of next 3 dc] 8 times, 2 dc in next dc, 1 dc in each of next 2 dc, join with sl st in ch 1. (45 sts)
Fasten off A and join B with sl st in ch 1 at beginning of round 5.
Round 6: Ch 1, [2 dc in next dc, 1 dc in each of next 4 dc] 8 times, 2 dc in next dc, 1 dc in each of next 3 dc, join with sl st in ch 1. (54 sts)
Round 7: Ch 1, [2 dc in next dc, 1 dc in each of next 5 dc] 8 times, 2 dc in next dc, 1 dc in each of next 4 dc, join with sl st in ch 1. (63 sts)
Round 8: Ch 1, [2 dc in next dc, 1 dc in each of next 6 dc] 8 times, 2 dc in next dc, 1 dc in each of next 5 dc, join with sl st in ch 1. (72 sts)
Fasten off.

PETALS (make 9)

Join C with sl st to first of any 2 dc in same place on round 8 and work each petal back and forth in rows as follows:
Row 1 (RS): Ch 1 (counts as 1 dc), 1 dc in each of next 8 dc, ending in first of next 2 dc in same place, turn. (9 sts)
Row 2: Ch 1, sk first dc, 1 dc in each of next 7 dc, 1 dc in ch 1, turn.
Row 3: As row 2.
Row 4: Ch 1, sk first dc, 1 dc in each remaining dc, turn leaving ch 1 unworked. (8 sts)
Repeat row 4 five more times. (3 sts)
Row 10: Ch 1, sk first dc, dc2tog over (next dc and ch 1).
Fasten off.
Repeat to make next petal, beginning in same dc of round 8 as final st of row 1 of petal just made. Continue all around, making nine petals in total.

54 *Starfish*
directory view pages 48 & 49

Yarn: Aran-weight wool in rust (A) and amber (B)
Size: Approx. 21cm (8¼in) diameter, using 4.5mm hook

METHOD
CENTRE DISC
Using A, ch 5 and join with sl st to form a ring. Work in a spiral as follows:

Round 1: 7 dc in ring.
Round 2: 2 dc in each dc. (14 sts)
Round 3: [2 dc in next dc, 1 dc in next dc] 7 times. (21 sts)
Round 4: [2 dc in next dc, 1 dc in each of next 2 dc] 7 times. (28 sts)
Round 5: [2 dc in next dc, 1 dc in each of next 3 dc] 7 times. (35 sts)
Round 6: 1 dc in each dc.
Round 7: [Dc2tog over next 2 dc, 1 dc in each of next 3 dc] 7 times. (28 sts)
Round 8: [Dc2tog over next 2 sts, 1 dc in each of next 2 dc] 7 times. (21 sts)
Round 9: [Dc2tog over next 2 sts, 1 dc in next dc] 7 times. (14 sts)
Round 10: [Dc2tog over next 2 sts] 7 times. (7 sts)
Fasten off with sl st in next st, leaving tail of yarn for sewing up.

PETALS (make 7)
Using B, make seven square-ended petals (see page 80).

FINISHING
Stuff centre disc with scraps of yarn A (or similar colour), then sew opening closed with tail of yarn, and at the same time stitch centre front and back of disc together to pull centre of sunflower in a little to shape it. Using B, sew straight edge of petals evenly spaced around back of disc.

Felted variation with no stuffing in centre disc.

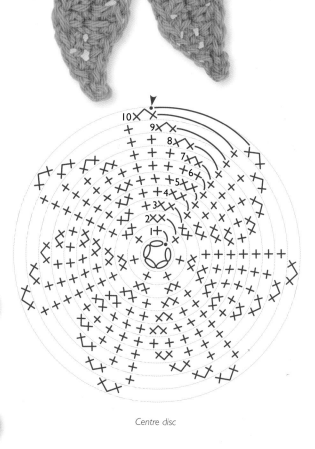

Centre disc

Ladybird
directory view page 41

Yarn: Aran-weight wool in black (A), red (B) and white (C)
Extras: Three hair grips for legs; round-nose pliers; glue suitable for use with metal
Size: Approx. 8cm (3¼in) long, using 4.5mm hook

METHOD

BODY (make 2)
Using A, ch 13.
Row 1: Sk first ch, 1 dc in each ch to end, turn. (12 dc)
Row 2: Ch 1, 1 dc in each dc to end, turn.
Row 3: Ch 1, 1 dc in first dc, 1 htr in each of next 2 dc, 2 tr in next dc, 1 tr in next dc, 2 dtr in next dc, 1 dtr in each of next 3 dc, 1 tr in next dc, 1 htr in each of next 2 dc, 1 dc in ch 1.
Continue along other side of foundation chain to make other side of body as follows:
Row 4: (1 dc, ch 1, 1 dc) in first ch made, 1 dc in of each of next 11 ch, turn.
Row 5: Ch 1, 1 dc in first dc, 1 htr in each of next 2 dc, 2 tr in next dc, 1 tr in next dc, 2 dtr in next dc, 1 dtr in each of next 3 dc, 1 tr in next dc, 1 htr in each of next 2 dc.
Fasten off with sl st in next ch.

WINGS (make 2)
Using B, ch 8.
Row 1: Skip first ch, 1 dc in each of next 7 dc.
Row 2: Ch 1, 1 dc in each dc to end, turn. (7 dc)
Row 3: Ch 3, 1 dtr in first dc, 2 dtr in next dc, 1 tr in next dc, 2 tr in next dc, 1 htr in each of next 2 dc, 1 dc in last dc, 1 dc in first ch made.
Fasten off.

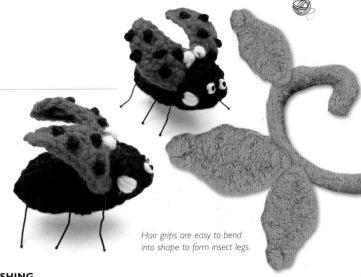

Hair grips are easy to bend into shape to form insect legs.

FINISHING
Using A, sew body pieces together, stuffing with scraps of yarn as you do so. Allow about one quarter of body length for head area. Sew wings to top of body behind head, attaching them only along the shorter straight edge and letting them flap open at centre back. Using double strand of A, work several French knots on each wing (see page 26). Using double strand of C, work a French knot at centre top of each wing and work several straight stitches to form a large spot at each side of head. Using single strand of C, work two French knots for eyes. Using single strand of A, stitch a small spot in middle of each eye. Use pliers to bend hair grips into the shape of three pairs of legs. Thread legs through body. To steady them, apply a small amount of glue to the points that join the crochet piece.

Use the photographs as a guide for working the embroidery stitches.

Body

Wing

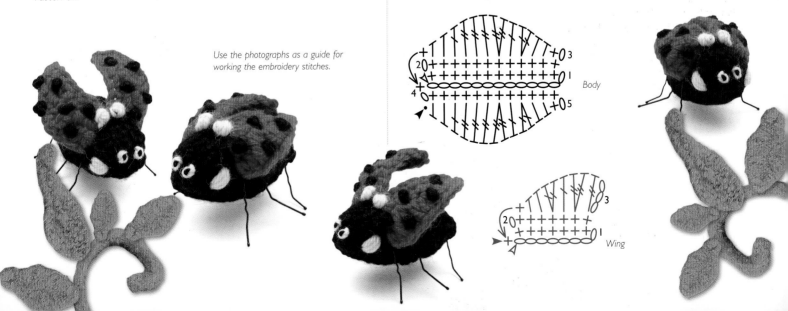

56 *Monarch Butterfly*
directory view page 49

Yarn: Aran-weight wool in black (A), orange (B), white (C) and gold (D)
Extras: Two 6mm (¹/₄in) round black beads for eyes; black sewing thread and needle; fabric glue (optional)
Size: Approx. 12cm (4³/₄in) square, using 4.5mm hook

METHOD
BODY
Using A, ch 2.
Row 1 (RS): Skip first ch, 2 dc in next ch, turn.
Row 2: Ch 1, 1 dc in first dc, 1 dc in next dc, 2 dc in ch 1, turn.
Row 3: Ch 1, sk first dc, 1 dc in each of next 3 dc, 1 dc in ch 1, turn.
Row 4: Ch 3, sk first dc, 1 tr in each of next 3 dc, 1 tr in ch 1, turn.
Row 5: Ch 3, 1 tr in first tr, 2 tr in each of next 2 tr, 1 tr in next tr, 1 tr in 3rd of ch 3, turn.
Row 6: Ch 1, sk first tr, 1 dc in next tr, 2 dc in next tr, 1 dc in each of next 2 tr, 2 dc in next tr, 1 dc in next tr, 1 dc in 3rd of ch 3, turn.
Row 7: Ch 1, sk first dc, 1 dc in each of next 8 dc, 1 dc in ch 1, turn.
Repeat row 7 three more times.
Row 11: Ch 1, sk first dc, [1 dc in next dc, sk next dc] 4 times, 1 dc in ch 1, turn.
Row 12: Ch 1, sk first dc, [1 dc in next dc, sk next dc] twice, 1 dc in ch 1. Fasten off with 1 dc in ch 1 at beginning of row 12.

WINGS
Using B, ch 5 and join with sl st to form a ring.
Round 1: Ch 3 (counts as 1 tr; place marker on this st), 13 tr in ring. (14 tr)
Upper right wing
Turn and work in rows as follows:
Row 1 (WS): Ch 2, 1 tr in tr at base of ch, 1 tr in each of next 2 tr, turn. (4 sts)
Row 2: Ch 2, 1 tr in first tr, 1 tr in each of next 2 tr, 2 tr in 2nd of ch 2, turn. (6 sts)
Row 3: Ch 2, sk first tr, 1 tr in each of next 4 tr, 1 tr in 2nd of ch 2, turn. (6 sts)
Row 4: Ch 1, 1 dc in first tr, 1 htr in next tr, 1 tr in each of next 2 tr, 2 dtr in next tr, 1 dtr in 2nd of ch 2. (7 sts)
Fasten off.
Upper left wing
With RS facing, rejoin B with sl st in top of 3rd tr of round 1. Turn and work in rows as follows:
Row 1 (WS): Ch 2, 1 tr in tr at base of ch, 1 tr in next tr, 1 tr in 3rd of ch 3, turn. (4 sts)
Rows 2–3: As for upper right wing.
Row 4: Ch 4 (counts as 1 dtr), sk first tr, 2 dtr in next tr, 1 tr in each of next 2 tr, 1 htr in next tr, 1 dc in 2nd of ch 2. (7 sts)
Fasten off.

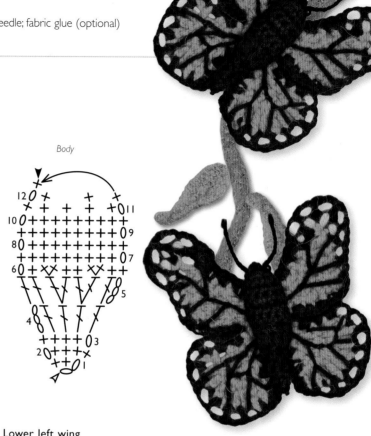

Body

Lower left wing
With RS facing, rejoin B with sl st in top of next (4th) tr of round 1. Do not turn. Work in rows as follows:
Row 1 (RS): Ch 2, 1 tr in tr at base of ch, 1 tr in each of next 2 tr, turn. (4 sts)
Row 2: Ch 2, 1 tr in first tr, 1 tr in each of next 2 tr, 2 tr in 2nd of ch 2, turn. (6 sts)
Row 3: Ch 2, sk first tr, 1 tr in next tr, 2 dtr in next tr, 3 dtr in next tr, 2 dtr in next tr, 2 tr in top of ch 2. (11 sts)
Fasten off.
Lower right wing
With RS facing, skip next 2 tr of round 1 and rejoin B with sl st in top of 9th tr of round 1. Do not turn. Work in rows as follows:
Rows 1–2: As for lower left wing.
Row 3: Ch 2, 1 tr in first tr, 2 dtr in next tr, 3 dtr in next tr, 2 dtr in next tr, 1 tr in next tr, 1 tr in 2nd of ch 2. (11 sts)
Fasten off.

WING EDGING

With RS facing, join A with sl st in 3rd of ch 3 at beg of round 1 (marked stitch).

Upper left wing

Work edging around upper left wing as follows: 2 dc in side of each of next 3 rows, (2 htr, 2 tr) in side of ch 4, (4 dtr, 1 tr) in 4th of ch 4 at top corner, (1 tr, 1 htr) in next dtr, [1 dc in space before next st] 5 times, 2 dc in last dc, 2 dc in side of each of next 3 rows.

Lower left wing

Continue around lower left wing: 2 dc in side of each of first 2 rows, 4 dc around ch 2 at beginning of row 3, sk next tr, [2 dc in space before next st] 6 times, [1 dc in space before next st] twice, 4 dc around last tr of row 3, 2 dc in side of each of next 2 rows, 1 dc in each of 2 skipped tr of round 1.

Lower right wing

Continue around lower right wing: 2 dc in side of each of next 2 rows, 4 dc around ch 2 at beginning of row 3, sk next tr, [1 dc in space before next st] twice, [2 dc in space before next st] 6 times, 4 dc around last tr of row 3, 2 dc in side of each of next 2 rows.

Upper right wing

Continue around upper right wing: 2 dc in side of each of next 3 rows, 1 dc in each of ch and dc at corner, [1 dc in space before next st] 5 times, (1 htr, 1 tr) in next dtr, (1 tr, 4 dtr) in last dtr at corner, (2 tr, 2 htr) in side of same dtr, 2 dc in side of next 3 rows.
Fasten off.

FINISHING

Using A, fold body in half lengthways and sew seam, stuffing body lightly with scraps of yarn as you do so. Sew body on to wings, centred over the round of tr. Join upper and lower wings for a short distance at each side of body. Using sewing thread, sew a bead at each side of head for eyes. Using single strand of A, add antennae at top of head, above the eyes (see page 23). Trim antennae to about 4cm (1½in) and stiffen with fabric glue if desired. Using double strand of C, work running stitch around outer edge of each wing (see page 26). Using double strand of D, work four random stitches at top of upper wings, just inside the white stitching. Using single strand of A, work long random stitches to simulate veins in butterfly wings.

Use the photographs as a guide for working the embroidery stitches.

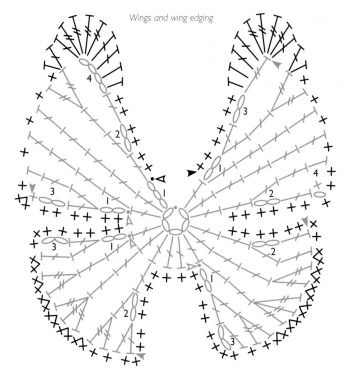

Wings and wing edging

PROJECTS

By this stage, you will probably have decided how you would like to use the designs that appeal to you the most, but if you have not, here are some suggestions for brightening, enlivening or just having fun adorning clothes, household objects and gifts.

PROJECT 1:
GIANT SUNFLOWER CUSHION

This realistic sunflower cushion is made by layering crochet petals around a sculpted centre disc embellished with embroidery, then applying the whole flower to a fabric cushion. For a larger sunflower, add one or more extra layers of petals.

MATERIALS
- Aran-weight wool yarn in orange (A), green (B), golden yellow (C) and dark brown (D)
- 5.5mm crochet hook
- Polyester toy stuffing
- 0.5m (1/2yd) yellow wool fabric for face of cushion
- 0.5m (1/2yd) orange cotton fabric for back of cushion
- Sewing needle and yellow thread

FINISHED SIZE
Approx. 30cm (12in) diameter

METHOD
CENTRE DISC
Using A, ch 4 and join with sl st to form a ring. Work in a spiral as follows:
Round 1: 5 dc in ring.
Round 2: 2 dc in each dc. (10 sts)
Round 3: [2 dc in next dc, 1 dc in next dc] 5 times. (15 sts)
Round 4: [2 dc in next dc, 1 dc in each of next 2 dc] 5 times. (20 sts)
Round 5: [2 dc in next dc, 1 dc in each of next 3 dc] 5 times. (25 sts)
Round 6: [2 dc in next dc, 1 dc in each of next 4 dc] 5 times. (30 sts)

Round 7: [2 dc in next dc, 1 dc in each of next 5 dc] 5 times. (35 sts)
Round 8: [2 dc in next dc, 1 dc in each of next 6 dc] 5 times. (40 sts)
Round 9: [2 dc in next dc, 1 dc in each of next 7 dc] 5 times. (45 sts)
Round 10: [2 dc in next dc, 1 dc in each of next 8 dc] 5 times. (50 sts)
Fasten off A and join B in same place.
Round 11: 1 dc in each dc.
Round 12: [2 dc in next dc, 1 dc in each of next 9 dc] 5 times. (55 sts)
Round 13: As round 11.
Round 14: [2 dc in next dc, 1 dc in each of next 10 dc] 5 times. (60 sts)
Round 15: [Sk next dc, 1 dc in each of next 9 dc] 6 times. (54 sts)
Round 16: [Sk next dc, 1 dc in each of next 8 dc] 6 times. (48 sts)
Round 17: [Sk next dc, 1 dc in each of next 7 dc] 6 times. (42 sts)
Fasten off.
Rounds 14–17 curve under, partially covering back of disc.

PETALS (MAKE 24)
Using C, make 24 large crochet petals (see page 80).

FINISHING
Using double strand of D, embroider French knots (see page 26) around front of centre disc where yarns A and B meet. Using C, sew base of twelve petals evenly spaced around back of centre disc. (Note: If you are using a single-spun yarn as in the sample, use a similar coloured plied yarn to attach the petals because the single-spun may unravel as you sew.) Sew base of remaining twelve petals around disc, positioning them behind the spaces between the first twelve petals. Stuff centre of flower with toy stuffing. Cut a circle of wool fabric 2.5cm (1in) larger all around than the flower. Cut a circle of backing fabric the same size. Place circles of fabric RS together and sew around them, using sewing thread and a 1.5cm (1/2in) seam allowance and leaving a 7.5cm (3in) opening. Turn RS out, press and stuff with more toy stuffing. Sew opening closed. Using sewing thread, sew flower on to front of cushion.

PROJECT 2: FARMERS' MARKET BAG

Shopping at your local farmers' market with a sunflower-decorated bag will brighten up everyone's day. This traditional basket bag lined with green fabric is embellished with a selection of flowers in a harmonious colour palette of yellows, oranges and greens. A honey bee gathering nectar from one of the flowers is the perfect finishing touch.

FEATURED DESIGNS
From left: Pompom Puff (see page 56), Prairie Gold (see page 59), Cocoa Sundrop (see page 56), Toffee Twist (see page 57), Giant Sungold (see page 54) and Honey Bee (see page 70), together with a selection of knit and crochet leaves (see pages 66–67 and 81). The flowers are attached with a few stitches threaded through the basketweave using matching yarn colours.

PROJECT 3: NAPKIN RINGS

Use a selection of flowers to make a set of unique napkin rings, perfect for a relaxed lunch or dinner party with family and friends. A sunflower napkin ring would also make a lovely gift for guests to take home with them afterwards.

MATERIALS
- Aran-weight wool yarn in pink (A), pale gold (B), green (C), dark brown (D), burnt orange (E), fuchsia (F) and bright orange (G)
- 4.5mm knitting needles
- 4.5mm crochet hook
- Small amount of green wool felt
- Sewing needle and green thread

METHOD
FLOWERS
Make a selection of small, flat sunflowers and felt them (see page 24). When dry, use a double strand of yarn to embroider French knots around the edge of each centre disc (see page 26). The flowers and colourways featured here are (above, clockwise from top left):
- **Pompom Gem** (see page 62), omitting the pompom and using A for petals, B for centre disc and alternating C and D for embroidery.

- **Small Teddy Bear** (see page 53), omitting stuffing and using C for rows 1–10, E for rows 11–17, D for rows 18–20 and B for embroidery.
- **Little Gem** (see page 75), using F for centre disc, B for petals and C for embroidery.
- **Raspberry Ruffle** (see page 78), using A for centre disc, G for petals, D for ruffle border and C for embroidery.

FINISHING
Cut four 5 x 15cm (2 x 6in) pieces of green wool felt. Pin the short ends together, overlapping by 6mm (¼in). Using sewing thread, sew the ends together to form a ring, then sew a flower to the top of each ring.

PROJECT 4:
SUMMER HAT

Make a sunny fashion statement by adorning your summer hat
with sunflowers. Here, a striking straw hat with bright red stripes is
embellished with a bold arrangement of sunflowers in toning shades of
red with highlights of green and orange. For a simpler look, you could
attach a single bloom with one or two leaves, or arrange a series of
small flowers all around the crown of the hat.

FEATURED DESIGNS
Three large Firecrackers (see page 53) worked in
Aran-weight yarn with deep red petals and brighter
red centre discs form a line from brim to crown of
hat. The arrangement is completed with a Pompom
Gem (see page 62) and Large Bud (see page 85),
together with several medium veined leaves with
short i-cord stems attached (see pages 66 and 64).
Either sew or pin the designs in place.

PROJECT 5: BABY RATTLE

Babies love to look at smiling faces. What sunflower doesn't make a person of any age smile? Combine the two – a smile and a sunflower – in a crochet flower made out of very soft cotton. Insert a noise-making ball and any baby will be entertained for hours.

MATERIALS
- Aran-weight cotton yarn in orange (A), yellow (B), lime green (C) and brown (D)
- 4mm crochet hook
- Noise-making ball, such as a rattle, cat toy or toy squeak
- Polyester toy stuffing

FINISHED SIZE
11.5cm (4½in) diameter

METHOD

CENTRE DISC
Using A, make a slip ring and work in a spiral as follows:
Round 1: 9 dc in ring.
Round 2: 2 dc in each dc. (18 sts)
Round 3: [2 dc in next dc, 1 dc in next dc] 9 times. (27 sts)
Round 4: [2 dc in next dc, 1 dc in each of next 2 dc] 9 times. (36 sts)
Round 5: [2 dc in next dc, 1 dc in each of next 3 dc] 9 times. (45 sts)
Rounds 6–9: 1 dc in each dc.
Round 10: [1 dc in each of next 4 dc, sk next dc] 9 times. (36 sts)
Round 11: [1 dc in each of next 3 dc, sk next dc] 9 times. (27 sts)
Insert noise-making ball and pack toy stuffing firmly around it.

Round 12: [1 dc in each of next 2 dc, sk next dc] 9 times. (18 sts)
Round 13: [1 dc in next dc, sk next dc] 9 times. (9 sts)
Fasten off.

PETALS (MAKE 13)
Using B, ch 6.
Row 1: Skip first ch, sl st in next ch, 1 dc in next ch, 1 htr in each of next 2 ch, 3 dc in last ch (base of petal). Continuing along other side of chain, 1 htr in each of next 2 ch, 1 dc in next ch. Fasten off with sl st at top of petal.

FLOWER BACK CONE
Using C, make a slip ring and work in a spiral as follows:
Round 1: 6 dc in ring.
Round 2: 2 dc in each dc. (12 sts)
Round 3: 1 dc in each dc.
Round 4: [2 dc in next dc, 1 dc in next dc] 6 times. (18 sts)
Round 5: [2 dc in next dc, 1 dc in each of next 2 dc] 6 times. (24 sts)
Round 6: [2 dc in next dc, 1 dc in each of next 3 dc] 6 times. (30 sts)
Round 7: 1 dc in each dc.
Fasten off, leaving 50cm (20in) tail.

STEM
Using C, make a crochet stem (see page 80) and sew the long edges together.

EYES (MAKE 2)
Using D, make a slip ring.
Round 1: 6 dc in ring, join with slip st in first dc. Pull starting yarn tail to tighten centre of ring. Fasten off, leaving 20cm (8in) tail.

SMILE
Using D, ch 12.
Row 1: Skip first ch, sl st in each chain to end. Fasten off, leaving 30cm (12in) tail.

FINISHING
Using tails of yarn, sew base of petals evenly spaced around back of centre disc, following one round of double crochet at the halfway point. Sew top of stem to back of flower back cone. Adding more toy stuffing around noise-making ball inside flower if necessary, stuff the flower back cone and then sew outer edge of cone to back of sunflower, overlapping attached edges of petals to hide them in the seam. Sew eyes and smile to front of flower. Make sure that you sew all components together very securely.

PROJECT 6:
MAIL BASKET

An ash-weave mail basket decorated with cheerful sunflowers could make even junk mail look attractive. This basket is embellished with a single large flower and leaf – Wagon Wheel (see page 55) and a bobble-edged leaf (see page 67) – but a bouquet of small flowers with stems would look just as good. The flowers can be glued in place or attached with a few stitches threaded through the woven strands of the basket using matching yarn colours.

PROJECT 7:
TEDDY BEAR BROOCH

Sungold sunflowers – also known as teddy bear sunflowers – are one of the most popular varieties to grow. Their puffy texture is so gorgeous in a vase, but also looks great on a jacket or sweater in the darkest days of winter. Make a Giant Sungold (see page 54) and felt it (see page 24). Using a sewing needle and matching thread, sew a brooch pin (available at craft shops) to the back edge of the flower. Sew an unfelted large teardrop leaf (see page 81) to the edge of the flower for additional textural interest.

PROJECT 8:
GRAPEVINE WREATH

Hang a grapevine wreath decorated with sunflowers on your door as the perfect welcome for guests to your home. Here, multiple flowers have been attached all around the wreath, but a simpler arrangement of two or three flowers at the base of the wreath would also look good. If using lots of flowers, repeating one of the designs several times (as done here) can help to balance the arrangement and showcase the other flowers.

FEATURED DESIGNS
Picot Star is used as the key flower in this arrangement. The two colourways shown on page 75 are complemented by four smaller versions worked in DK-weight yarn in gold with burgundy petals. The designs featured on this wreath are (clockwise from top): Monarch Butterfly (see page 94), Picot Star, Sunbright (see page 79), two Picot Stars, Lazy Daisy (see page 61) and three Picot Stars. The flowers are set against a selection of knit and crochet leaves (see pages 66–67 and 81), with a long i-cord stem (see page 64) twisting around the wreath below them. A felted i-cord stem (see page 24) tied in a knot is used to hang the wreath.

PROJECT 9:
POLKA DOT VASE

This cute little vase involves working around a glass jar to enclose it in a crochet cover. The felted flowers are both knit and crochet. The felting process makes the flowers look softer, although in fact it makes them firmer and more sculptural. Almost all of the flowers in this book could be treated in a similar manner.

MATERIALS

- Aran-weight wool yarn in blue (A), ecru (B), green (C), orange (D), dark brown (E), pink (F) and pale gold (G)
- 4mm crochet hook for vase
- 5.5mm crochet hook and 5.5mm knitting needles for flowers
- Two 4.5mm double-pointed knitting needles for i-cord
- Glass jar such as 1-litre (quart-size) mason jar
- Small amount of polyester toy stuffing
- Craft glue
- 6mm (¼in) clear vinyl tubing (available at DIY and plumbing supply stores)
- 1mm (18-gauge) stainless steel wire
- Wire cutters and round-nose pliers
- Sewing needle and green thread

SIZE OF VASE

Approx. 17cm (6¾in) high x 9.5cm (3¾in) diameter base

METHOD

VASE

Using A, ch 4 and join with sl st to form a ring. Work in a spiral as follows:

Round 1: 5 dc in ring.
Round 2: 2 dc in each dc. (10 sts)
Round 3: [2 dc in next dc, 1 dc in next dc] 5 times. (15 sts)
Round 4: [2 dc in next dc, 1 dc in each of next 2 dc] 5 times. (20 sts)
Round 5: [2 dc in next dc, 1 dc in each of next 3 dc] 5 times. (25 sts)
Round 6: [2 dc in next dc, 1 dc in each of next 4 dc] 5 times. (30 sts)
Round 7: [2 dc in next dc, 1 dc in each of next 5 dc] 5 times. (35 sts)
Round 8: [2 dc in next dc, 1 dc in each of next 6 dc] 5 times. (40 sts)
Round 9: [2 dc in next dc, 1 dc in each of next 7 dc] 5 times. (45 sts)
Round 10: [2 dc in next dc, 1 dc in each of next 8 dc] 5 times. (50 sts)
This completes base of vase. Begin working straight sides as follows:
Rounds 11–22: 1 dc in each dc.
Increase to shape bulbous section as follows:
Round 23: [2 dc in next dc, 1 dc in each of next 9 dc] 5 times. (55 sts)

Rounds 24–27: 1 dc in each dc.
Round 28: [2 dc in next dc, 1 dc in each of next 4 dc] 11 times. (66 sts)
Round 29: 1 dc in each dc.
Repeat round 29 if necessary to fit glass jar.
Slip glass jar inside crochet. Carefully arrange a layer of stuffing around the bulbous section between the vase and the glass jar.
Work around glass jar while decreasing for top of vase as follows:
Round 30: [Dc2tog, 1 dc in each of next 9 dc] 6 times. (60 sts)
Round 31: [Dc2tog, 1 dc in each of next 8 dc] 6 times. (54 sts)
Round 32: [Dc2tog, 1 dc in each of next 7 dc] 6 times. (48 sts)
Round 33: [Dc2tog, 1 dc in each of next 6 dc] 6 times. (42 sts)
Round 34: [Dc2tog, 1 dc in each of next 5 dc] 6 times. (36 sts)
Round 35: [Dc2tog, 1 dc in each of next 4 dc] 6 times. (30 sts)
Round 36: [Dc2tog, 1 dc in each of next 3 dc] 6 times. (24 sts)
Rounds 37–42: 1 dc in each dc.
Work top rim edging as follows:
Round 43: [2 dc in next dc, 1 dc in next dc] 12 times. (36 sts)
Round 44: 2 dc in each dc. (72 sts)
Round 45: 1 dc in each dc.
Fasten off.

POLKA DOTS

This vase has 5 large and 6 small polka dots, but you can make as many as you want.
Using B, make a slip ring and work in a spiral as follows:
Round 1: 5 dc in ring.
Pull starting yarn tail to tighten centre of ring.
Round 2: 2 dc in each dc. (10 sts)
Fasten off here for small dot, or work round 3 for large dot as follows:
Round 3: [2 dc in next dc, 1 dc in next dc] 5 times. (15 sts)
Fasten off.
Steam the dots flat and allow to dry completely. Using craft glue, glue the polka dots randomly on to the vase.

FLOWER COMPONENTS

Make all of the flower components, but keep the flowers, flower back cones, stems and leaves separate until after felting. The flowers featured here are (from left):

- **Starfish** (see page 92), using E for centre disc and D for petals. Finish as described but do not stuff centre disc. Using C, make a crochet cone for the flower back, increasing to finish with 30 sts on last round (see page 80), and two medium teardrop leaves (see page 81).
- **Swizzle Sticks** (see page 59), using D for top layer of petals, F for middle layer of petals and G for centre disc. Omit bottom layer of petals and finish as described. Using C, make a knitted cone for the flower back, casting off after row 11 (see page 64); sew seam of cone, making sure that you leave an opening at the base. Using C, make two medium veined leaves (see page 66).
- **Bobble Beauty** (see page 62), using D for bobbles (rows 1–3 of centre disc), E for remainder of centre disc, G for petals and finishing as described. Using C, make a knitted cone for the flower back and two leaves as for Swizzle Sticks.
- Using C, make three i-cord stems (see page 64), casting on 6 sts and making each stem 20–25cm (8–10in) long.

FLOWER ASSEMBLY

For each stem, cut a piece of vinyl tubing, about 20cm (8in) longer than the stem. Insert the tube into the stem so that 10cm (4in) hangs out at each end. Felt all of the flower components (see page 24) and allow to dry completely. For each stem, push the tubing down inside the i-cord at one end, and insert two pieces of wire into the tube. Fold 13mm (½in) of the wire over the top of the tube to catch and secure the felted stem. Insert the stem through a flower back cone so that the stem extends to the front of the cone. Use sewing thread to stitch the stem in place. For each flower, stuff the cone with scraps of yarn C or toy stuffing and sew to back of flower, then sew the leaves to top of stem. Place flowers in vase and trim bottom of wire and tubing to required height. Bend the stems to your liking.

PROJECT 10: POTHOLDERS

There is nothing better than a wool potholder; wool resists burning and is a great insulator. Made from tweed wool fabric for a rustic feel, the crochet sunflowers were felted before being applied to the fabric. A line of chain stitch embroidery defines the centre of the flowers.

MATERIALS
- Aran-weight tweed wool yarn in pale yellow (A), orange (B) and dark brown (C)
- 6.5mm crochet hook
- Plate or bowl of diameter required for potholders
- 23cm (¼yd) tweed wool fabric (adjust quantity to suit size of potholders you are making)
- Sewing needle and yellow, orange and brown thread

FINISHED SIZE
Approx. 21cm (8¼in) diameter

METHOD

FLOWERS (MAKE 2)
Make two Picot Stars (see page 75), using A for centre disc and B for petals on first flower, and vice versa on second flower. Felt the flowers (see page 24) and allow to dry completely. Using double strand of C, embroider a circle of chain stitch around edge of centre discs (see page 26).

FINISHING
Find a plate or bowl in an appropriate size for a potholder – the one used for this pair was 21cm (8¼in) diameter. Trace on a piece of paper to make a circle template. For each potholder, use the template to cut out two pieces of wool fabric. Cut a 2 × 7.5cm (¾ × 3in) strip of fabric to make a tab. Pin a felted flower to the RS of one circle. Using sewing needle and thread to match the petal colour, sew the flower in place with small stitches around the edges of the petals; the stitches will disappear into the felted flower. Pin the two circles of fabric WS together, enclosing the ends of the folded tab between the circles. Sew together, using brown thread and a 1cm (³⁄₈in) seam allowance.

PROJECT 11:
SEW-ON FLOWER CUSHIONS

Liven up some plain cushions by decorating them with sunflowers. Sew a selection of knit and crochet sunflowers, stems and leaves randomly on to the front of a cushion, or make a bold statement with a single large bloom in a vibrant colour scheme. Use sewing thread in matching colours to attach the flowers, making sure that the ends of stems are tucked under them. Take care to keep the back of the cushion loose from the front when sewing.

FEATURED DESIGNS
Orange cushion (clockwise from top left): blocked Raspberry Ruffle (see page 78), Sweet Petite (see page 60), Swizzle Sticks (see page 59), unblocked Raspberry Ruffle, Crème Caramel (see page 54), Openwork Star (see page 84), Bobble Beauty (see page 62) and Catherine Wheel (see page 63). The flowers are linked by a long i-cord stem (see page 64) and embellished with a selection of knit and crochet leaves (see pages 66–67 and 81).
Green cushion: Amethyst Queen (see page 63), two extra large leaves with picot edging (see page 81) and a felted i-cord stem (see pages 64 and 24).

PROJECT 12: WASHCLOTH

This project makes a perfect hostess gift when packaged with a handmade bar of soap. It is fun to knit and very quick to make. Knit up a few and keep them on hand, to use as gifts for any occasion.

MATERIALS
- Aran-weight kitchen cotton yarn in yellow (A), orange (B) and lime green (C)
- 4.5mm knitting needles

FINISHED SIZE
Approx. 22cm (8¾in) diameter

METHOD
PETALS (MAKE 13)
Using A, cast on 7 sts and make a strip of petals as for the Wagon Wheel sunflower (see page 55), but with 13 petals rather than 11.

CENTRE DISC
Hold petal strip with unattached ends of petals hanging down. Using B and with RS facing, pick up and knit 6 sts from base of each petal along top edge of strip. (78 sts)
Row 1 (WS): Knit.
Row 2: [K2, k2tog] 19 times, k2. (59 sts)
Row 3: Knit.
Row 4: [K1, k2tog] 19 times, k2. (40 sts)

Row 5: Knit.
Break off B and join C.
Row 6: [K1, k2tog] 13 times, k1. (27 sts)
Row 7: Knit.
Row 8: [K1, k2tog] 9 times (18 sts)
Row 9: Knit.
Row 10: [K2tog] 9 times. (9 sts)
Break off yarn, leaving 20cm (8in) tail. Thread tail into a yarn needle and pass through remaining 9 sts. Tighten to close centre of disc, then sew side edges of disc together to form a circle.

FINISHING
Wash and dry the washcloth in a washing machine and dryer, following the yarn manufacturer's directions. This process will make the stitches more even and soften the washcloth.

PROJECT 13:
WALL ART

You don't have to be Van Gogh to create a sunflower masterpiece worth hanging on your wall. Simple white box frames containing black-and-white pictures of old sunflower engravings provide the perfect backdrop for a selection of brightly coloured blooms. Look on the internet for similar out-of-copyright sunflower images to print at home, or photocopy them from old books of engravings. The flowers are attached using double-sided sticky tape, so you can easily change the display whenever you wish.

FEATURED DESIGNS
Large frame (clockwise from top left quarter): Crème Caramel (see page 54) and Little Gem (see page 75); Little Gem and Small Teddy Bear (see page 53); Small Bud (see page 85) and Sea Anemone (see page 84); Picot Star (see page 75) and Little Gem.
Small frame: Sweet Petite (see page 60) and unblocked Raspberry Ruffle (see page 78).
Both frames also feature a selection of knit and crochet petals and leaves (see pages 66–67 and 80–81).

PROJECT 14:
LAMPSHADE

This simple jute lampshade is decorated with sunflowers made from shiny mercerised cotton yarn. When lit, the flower shapes make shadows in the light. Knitted flowers have been used here, but crochet ones would look just as good. It is advisable to treat the finished lampshade with a suitable fire-retardant spray.

MATERIALS

- DK-weight mercerised cotton yarn in orange (A), yellow (B), dark brown (C), bright green (D), gold (E), toffee (F) and mid-green (G)
- 4.5mm knitting needles
- Jute fabric lampshade; this one is approx. 30cm (12in) diameter x 23cm (9in) high
- Craft glue
- Fire-retardant spray suitable for cotton textiles

METHOD

FLOWERS

Choose flat sunflowers rather than three-dimensional designs. The number required will depend on the size of the flowers you choose and the size of the lampshade. The flowers featured here are (above, from left):

- **Crème Caramel** (see page 54), using A for petals, C for row 1 of centre disc and D for remainder of centre disc.
- **Cocoa Sundrop** (see page 56), using E for petals, C for centre disc and double strand of D for French knot embroidery around edge of centre disc.
- **Joker** (see page 57), using C for centre disc, A for long petals, B for frilled petals and double strand of D for French knot embroidery around edge of centre disc (see page 26).
- **Bobble Beauty** (see page 62), using B for bobbles (rows 1–3 of centre disc), D for remainder of centre disc and F for petals.

STEMS

Using G, cast on enough sts for length of stem required for your lampshade (here, one stem has 10 sts, one has 15 sts and two have 25 sts each).
Knit two rows, then cast off.

LEAVES

Using G, make pairs of veined leaves to place at the base of some of the stems (see page 66). Here, two medium leaves are used below Crème Caramel and two thin leaves below Bobble Beauty. No leaves are used below Cocoa Sundrop or Joker.

FINISHING

Block and steam the flowers, stems and leaves to flatten them. When completely dry, use craft glue to attach the flowers to the lampshade, with a stem and leaves (if desired) below each flower. Treat the lampshade with a suitable fire-retardant spray, following the manufacturer's directions.

PROJECT 15:
APPLIQUÉ CARDIGAN

When time doesn't allow for making an entirely handknit or crochet cardigan for a new baby or small child, dress up a store-bought version. Crochet sunflowers, stems and leaves are sewn on with a large, decorative running stitch in a contrasting colour. The effect is that of handmade but it will only take you a couple of hours.

MATERIALS
- Aran-weight cotton/wool blend yarn in purple (A), yellow (B), green (C) and lavender (D)
- 3.5mm and 4.5mm crochet hooks
- Child's cotton cardigan
- Tapestry needle and light green and dark green cotton embroidery thread

METHOD
FLOWERS (MAKE 2)
Using 3.5mm hook, make two Little Gem sunflowers (see page 75), using A for centre disc and B for petals on first flower, and vice versa on second flower.

STEMS (MAKE 1 SHORT AND 1 LONG)
Using 4.5mm hook and C, ch 20 for short stem or ch 30 for long stem.
Row 1: Sk first ch, 1 dc in each ch to end.
Fasten off.

LEAVES (MAKE 7)
Using 4.5mm hook and D, make seven small teardrop leaves (see page 81).

FINISHING
Pin flowers, stems and leaves to cardigan, referring to photograph for placement. Using a tapestry needle and double strand of light green embroidery thread, sew stems in place with a line of running stitch along centre of each stem (see page 26). Using double strand of dark green embroidery thread, attach a flower at top of each stem with running stitch around edge of centre disc. Still using dark green thread, sew leaves to right and left of each stem with running stitch just inside the edges of each leaf.

INDEX

RESOURCES

Giant sunflower cushion (p98):
Valley Yarns Berkshire (85% wool, 15% alpaca; approx. 129m [141yds] per 100g skein); 1 skein each in A (Orange 12) & B (Mistletoe 37), 2 skeins in C (Gold 10), small amount in D (Coffee Bean 39)

Napkin rings (p102): Classic Elite Yarns Color by Kristin (50% wool, 25% mohair, 25% alpaca; approx. 85m [93yds] per 50g ball); 1 ball each in A (Julia's Pink 3289), B (Yarrow 3243), C (Spring Green 3215), D (French Roast 3276), E (October Leaves 3278), F (Raspberry 3232) & G (Pumpkin 3285)

Baby rattle (p106): Lily Sugar'n Cream (100% cotton; approx. 109m [120yds] per 70g skein); 1 skein each in A (Tangerine 01699), B (Yellow 00010), C (Hot Green 01712) & D (Terra Firma 02013)

Teddy bear brooch (p109): Valley Yarns Northampton (100% wool; approx. 226m [247yds] per 100g skein); 1 skein each in A (Gold 15) & B (Apple Green 10)

Polka dot vase (p112): Classic Elite Yarns Color by Kristin (50% wool, 25% alpaca, 25% mohair; approx. 85m [93yds] per 50g ball); 2 balls in A (Cornflower Blue 3257), 1 ball each in B (Natural 3216), C (Spring Green 3215), D (Pumpkin 3285), E (French Roast 3276), F (Julia's Pink 3289) & G (Yarrow 3243)

Potholders (p114): Tahki Yarns Donegal Tweed (100% wool; approx. 167m [183yds] per 100g skein); 1 skein each in A (Goldenrod 882) & B (Burnt Orange 873), small amount in C (Dark Chocolate 833)

Washcloth (p118): Lily Sugar'n Cream (100% cotton; approx. 109m [120yds] per 70g skein); 1 ball each in A (Yellow 00100), B (Tangerine 01699) & C (Hot Green 01712)

Lampshade (p122): Kertzer Super-10 Butterfly Cotton (100% mercerised cotton; approx. 230m [250yds] per 125g hank); 1 hank each in A (Tangerine 3402), B (Canary 3553), C (Mocha 3214), D (Lime 3724), E (Goldenrod 5020), F (Ginger 3358) & G (Pistachio 3717)

Appliqué cardigan (p124): Classic Elite Yarns Chesapeake (50% organic cotton, 50% merino wool; approx. 94m [103yds] per 50g skein); 1 skein each in A (Rosetti Purple 5995), B (Meyer Lemon 5912), C (Sage Green 5987) & D (Lavender 5956)

PICTURE CREDITS

Quarto would like to acknowledge and thank the following for kindly supplying images reproduced in this book:

• Kristin Nicholas (pp29 & 30 sunflower photographs): www.kristinnicholas.com & getting-stitched-on-the-farm.blogspot.com

• Shutterstock.com: / Robyn Mackenzie & Madlen (p31 leaves); / Oleg Golovnev & rook76 (p108 sunflower postage stamps); / detibarto, Hein Nouwens & Evelyn Sichrovsky (pp120 & 121 framed sunflower images)

easigrass™
the artificial grass company

Thanks also to easigrass for supplying the grass background featured in the directory: www.easigrass.com 0845 094 8880

All other photographs and illustrations are the copyright of Quarto Publishing plc. While every effort has been made to credit contributors, Quarto would like to apologise should there have been any omissions or errors – and would be pleased to make the appropriate correction for future editions of the book.

AUTHOR'S ACKNOWLEDGEMENTS

Thanks to my Mom and Dad – Arch and Nancy Nicholas – for instilling in me their love of gardening and flowers. Thanks to my agent Linda Roghaar for her encouragement, and to BJ Berti for seeing the potential in this project. Thanks to all the fine folks at Quarto for producing the colourful book that you hold in your hands. Thanks so much to the yarn companies who supplied their beautiful fibres, including Classic Elite Yarns, Westminster Fibers, Valley Yarns, Tahki/Stacy Charles, Lion Brand and Universal Yarns.

Many thanks to all my loyal 'Getting Stitched on the Farm' blog readers, who continue to encourage my art and craft. Lastly, love to my husband Mark Duprey for growing that first field of colourful sunflowers many years ago, and to my daughter Julia whose smiling face and sunny disposition continues to be the bright spot in my day.

ENGLISH/AMERICAN TERMINOLOGY

The patterns in this book use English terminology, which differs somewhat from American terminology. You may find this list of English terms and their American equivalents useful.

ENGLISH	AMERICAN
double crochet (dc)	single crochet (sc)
half treble crochet (htr)	half double crochet (hdc)
treble crochet (tr)	double crochet (dc)
double treble crochet (dtr)	treble crochet (tr)
triple treble crochet (ttr or trtr)	double treble crochet (dtr)